50 Vegan Bowl Recipes for Home

By: Kelly Johnson

Table of Contents

- Quinoa Black Bean Bowl
- Lentil Curry Bowl
- Teriyaki Tofu Bowl
- Mediterranean Chickpea Bowl
- BBQ Jackfruit Bowl
- Thai Peanut Noodle Bowl
- Mexican Rice Bowl
- Falafel Bowl
- Sweet Potato and Kale Bowl
- Coconut Curry Bowl
- Sushi Bowl
- Moroccan Couscous Bowl
- Greek Salad Bowl
- Avocado and Black Bean Bowl
- Roasted Veggie Quinoa Bowl
- Lemon Herb Tempeh Bowl
- Vegan Bibimbap Bowl
- Butternut Squash Buddha Bowl
- Edamame and Brown Rice Bowl
- Chickpea Shawarma Bowl
- Vegan Caesar Salad Bowl
- Ratatouille Bowl
- Buffalo Cauliflower Bowl
- Pesto Pasta Bowl
- Green Goddess Bowl
- Burrito Bowl
- Sesame Ginger Noodle Bowl
- Spicy Peanut Tempeh Bowl
- Mediterranean Orzo Bowl
- Korean BBQ Tofu Bowl
- Portobello Fajita Bowl
- Beet and Quinoa Bowl
- Thai Green Curry Bowl
- Harvest Grain Bowl
- Vegan Taco Salad Bowl

- Mango Salsa Rice Bowl
- Caprese Salad Bowl
- Mexican Street Corn Bowl
- Spinach and Artichoke Quinoa Bowl
- Hawaiian Poke Bowl
- Balsamic Glazed Veggie Bowl
- Cauliflower Shawarma Bowl
- Sesame Orange Tofu Bowl
- Ratatouille Polenta Bowl
- Coconut Lime Rice Bowl
- Vegan Cobb Salad Bowl
- Chipotle Sweet Potato Bowl
- Mediterranean Stuffed Pepper Bowl
- Teriyaki Mushroom Bowl
- Curried Chickpea Couscous Bowl

Quinoa Black Bean Bowl

Ingredients:

- 1 cup quinoa, rinsed
- 2 cups water or vegetable broth
- 1 can (15 oz) black beans, drained and rinsed
- 1 red bell pepper, diced
- 1 small red onion, finely chopped
- 1 cup corn kernels (fresh, frozen, or canned)
- 1 avocado, sliced
- Fresh cilantro, chopped (for garnish)
- Lime wedges (for serving)
- Salt and pepper, to taste

For the dressing:

- 3 tablespoons olive oil
- 2 tablespoons lime juice
- 1 teaspoon ground cumin
- 1 teaspoon chili powder
- Salt and pepper, to taste

Instructions:

1. Cook the Quinoa:
   - In a medium saucepan, combine the quinoa and water or vegetable broth. Bring to a boil over medium-high heat.
   - Reduce the heat to low, cover, and simmer for 15-20 minutes, or until the quinoa is cooked and the liquid is absorbed. Remove from heat and let it sit covered for 5 minutes. Fluff with a fork.
2. Prepare the Dressing:
   - In a small bowl, whisk together the olive oil, lime juice, ground cumin, chili powder, salt, and pepper. Set aside.
3. Assemble the Bowl:
   - In a large mixing bowl, combine the cooked quinoa, black beans, diced bell pepper, chopped red onion, and corn kernels.
   - Pour the dressing over the quinoa mixture and toss until everything is well combined and evenly coated with the dressing.
4. Serve:
   - Divide the quinoa black bean mixture into serving bowls.
   - Top each bowl with sliced avocado.

- Garnish with fresh cilantro and serve with lime wedges on the side.
- Season with additional salt and pepper if needed.

Enjoy your delicious and nutritious Quinoa Black Bean Bowl!

Lentil Curry Bowl

Ingredients:

- 1 cup dried lentils (green or brown), rinsed
- 3 cups vegetable broth or water
- 1 onion, finely chopped
- 3 cloves garlic, minced
- 1 tablespoon fresh ginger, grated
- 1 tablespoon curry powder
- 1 teaspoon ground cumin
- 1 teaspoon ground turmeric
- 1/2 teaspoon paprika (optional)
- 1 can (14 oz) diced tomatoes
- 1 can (14 oz) coconut milk
- Salt and pepper, to taste
- Cooked rice or quinoa, for serving
- Fresh cilantro, chopped (for garnish)
- Lime wedges (for serving)

Optional Additions:

- Sliced bell peppers
- Spinach or kale
- Cubed potatoes or sweet potatoes
- Cauliflower florets

Instructions:

1. Cook the Lentils:
    - In a saucepan, combine the rinsed lentils with vegetable broth or water. Bring to a boil over medium-high heat.
    - Reduce the heat to low, cover, and simmer for about 20-25 minutes or until the lentils are tender. Drain any excess liquid and set aside.
2. Prepare the Curry:
    - In a large skillet or pot, heat a bit of oil over medium heat.
    - Add the chopped onion and sauté for 5-6 minutes until softened.
    - Stir in the minced garlic and grated ginger, and cook for another minute until fragrant.
3. Add Spices:
    - Add the curry powder, ground cumin, turmeric, and paprika (if using) to the skillet. Stir well to coat the onions and spices.
4. Combine with Tomatoes and Coconut Milk:

- Pour in the diced tomatoes with their juices and coconut milk. Stir to combine everything.
- Bring the mixture to a simmer and let it cook for 10-15 minutes to allow the flavors to meld together and the sauce to thicken slightly.
5. Add Cooked Lentils and Adjust Seasoning:
    - Add the cooked lentils to the curry sauce. Stir well to combine.
    - Taste and season with salt and pepper as needed.
6. Optional Additions:
    - If using additional vegetables like bell peppers, spinach, or potatoes, add them to the curry during the last 10 minutes of cooking until they are tender.
7. Serve:
    - Serve the lentil curry over cooked rice or quinoa in bowls.
    - Garnish with chopped fresh cilantro and serve with lime wedges on the side.

Enjoy your hearty and delicious Lentil Curry Bowl packed with protein and aromatic spices!

Teriyaki Tofu Bowl

Ingredients:

For the Teriyaki Tofu:

- 1 block (14-16 oz) firm tofu, drained and pressed
- 1/4 cup soy sauce (or tamari for gluten-free option)
- 2 tablespoons maple syrup or brown sugar
- 2 tablespoons rice vinegar
- 2 cloves garlic, minced
- 1 teaspoon grated ginger
- 1 tablespoon cornstarch
- 2 tablespoons water
- Sesame seeds, for garnish

For the Bowl:

- Cooked rice (white, brown, or sushi rice)
- Steamed or stir-fried vegetables (broccoli, carrots, bell peppers, snap peas, etc.)
- Sliced green onions, for garnish
- Optional toppings: sliced avocado, shredded cabbage, edamame, or pickled ginger

Instructions:

1. Prepare the Tofu:
    - Press the block of tofu to remove excess water. You can do this by wrapping the tofu in paper towels or a clean kitchen towel and placing a heavy object (like a cast iron skillet) on top for 15-30 minutes. Then, cut the tofu into cubes or slices.
2. Make the Teriyaki Sauce:
    - In a small bowl, whisk together soy sauce, maple syrup (or brown sugar), rice vinegar, minced garlic, and grated ginger to make the teriyaki sauce.
3. Cook the Tofu:
    - Heat a non-stick skillet or wok over medium-high heat. Add a bit of oil.

- Add the tofu cubes to the hot pan and cook until golden and crispy on all sides, about 5-7 minutes.
4. Add the Teriyaki Sauce:
    - Once the tofu is crispy, pour the teriyaki sauce over the tofu in the pan. Stir gently to coat the tofu with the sauce.
    - In a small bowl, mix cornstarch and water to create a slurry. Add this mixture to the pan with the tofu and sauce. Stir well and cook for another 1-2 minutes until the sauce thickens and coats the tofu.
5. Assemble the Teriyaki Tofu Bowl:
    - Divide cooked rice among serving bowls.
    - Top the rice with the teriyaki tofu and steamed or stir-fried vegetables of your choice.
    - Garnish with sliced green onions and sesame seeds.
6. Optional Toppings:
    - Feel free to customize your bowl with additional toppings like sliced avocado, shredded cabbage, edamame, or pickled ginger.
7. Serve and Enjoy:
    - Serve the Teriyaki Tofu Bowl immediately while hot.
    - Enjoy the savory-sweet flavors of the teriyaki tofu combined with rice and vegetables!

This Teriyaki Tofu Bowl is a delicious and satisfying vegan meal that's perfect for lunch or dinner. Adjust the seasonings and toppings to your liking for a personalized bowl.

BBQ Jackfruit Bowl

Ingredients:

For the BBQ Jackfruit:

- 2 cans young green jackfruit in water or brine, drained and rinsed
- 1 tablespoon olive oil
- 1 small onion, finely chopped
- 2 cloves garlic, minced
- 1 cup barbecue sauce
- Salt and pepper, to taste

For the Bowl:

- Cooked rice or quinoa
- Black beans, drained and rinsed
- Corn kernels (fresh or canned)
- Sliced avocado
- Cherry tomatoes, halved
- Fresh cilantro, chopped
- Lime wedges

Instructions:

1. Prepare the BBQ Jackfruit:

   1. Prep Jackfruit: Rinse and drain the jackfruit. Pat dry and remove any seeds or tough core parts.
   2. Sauté: Heat olive oil in a skillet over medium heat. Add chopped onions and garlic, sauté until softened and fragrant.
   3. Add Jackfruit: Add the jackfruit to the skillet. Use a fork or potato masher to break up the jackfruit into shreds.
   4. Cook with BBQ Sauce: Pour the barbecue sauce over the jackfruit. Stir well to combine. Cook for 8-10 minutes, stirring occasionally, until the jackfruit is heated through and has absorbed the flavors. Add salt and pepper to taste.

2. Assemble the Bowl:

   1. Base: Start with a base of cooked rice or quinoa in each serving bowl.
   2. Add Toppings: Arrange the BBQ jackfruit on top of the rice. Add black beans, corn kernels, sliced avocado, and cherry tomatoes around the bowl.

3. Garnish: Sprinkle fresh cilantro over the bowl. Serve with lime wedges on the side for squeezing over the bowl before eating.

3. Serve and Enjoy:

- Serve the BBQ Jackfruit Bowl immediately, allowing each person to squeeze fresh lime juice over their bowl before enjoying.
- Feel free to customize the toppings based on your preferences. Other great additions could include shredded lettuce, diced red onion, jalapeños, or a drizzle of vegan sour cream.

This BBQ Jackfruit Bowl is not only packed with flavor but also offers a satisfying combination of textures and nutrients. It's perfect for a quick and healthy weeknight dinner or a weekend lunch. Enjoy!

Thai Peanut Noodle Bowl

Ingredients:

For the Peanut Sauce:

- 1/2 cup creamy peanut butter
- 3 tablespoons soy sauce (or tamari for gluten-free)
- 2 tablespoons rice vinegar
- 2 tablespoons lime juice
- 2 tablespoons brown sugar or maple syrup
- 2 cloves garlic, minced
- 1 teaspoon grated fresh ginger
- 1/2 teaspoon sriracha or chili garlic sauce (adjust to taste)
- 1/3 cup warm water (more as needed to thin the sauce)

For the Noodle Bowl:

- 8 ounces rice noodles or any noodles of your choice
- 1 tablespoon sesame oil
- 1 red bell pepper, thinly sliced
- 1 carrot, julienned or thinly sliced
- 1 cup shredded purple cabbage
- 1 cup edamame (cooked and shelled)
- Sliced green onions, for garnish
- Chopped fresh cilantro, for garnish
- Crushed peanuts, for garnish (optional)
- Lime wedges, for serving

Instructions:

1. Prepare the Peanut Sauce:
    1. In a bowl, whisk together peanut butter, soy sauce, rice vinegar, lime juice, brown sugar (or maple syrup), minced garlic, grated ginger, and sriracha until smooth.
    2. Gradually add warm water to thin out the sauce to your desired consistency. Set aside.

2. Cook the Noodles:
    1. Cook the rice noodles according to package instructions. Drain and rinse under cold water to stop cooking. Toss with sesame oil to prevent sticking and set aside.

3. Assemble the Noodle Bowl:
    1. In a large mixing bowl, combine cooked noodles, sliced bell pepper, julienned carrot, shredded cabbage, and edamame.

2. Pour the prepared peanut sauce over the noodles and vegetables. Toss well to coat everything evenly with the sauce.

4. Serve and Garnish:

   1. Divide the Thai peanut noodle mixture into serving bowls.
   2. Garnish each bowl with sliced green onions, chopped cilantro, and crushed peanuts (if using).
   3. Serve with lime wedges on the side for squeezing over the noodles.

5. Enjoy!

   - Serve the Thai Peanut Noodle Bowls immediately, either warm or chilled.
   - Feel free to customize this dish with additional vegetables like cucumber, snow peas, or bean sprouts, and add grilled tofu, cooked shrimp, or shredded chicken for extra protein.

This Thai Peanut Noodle Bowl is a delightful and satisfying meal that's perfect for lunch or dinner.

The creamy peanut sauce combined with the crunchy vegetables and noodles creates a wonderful texture and flavor experience. Enjoy!

Mexican Rice Bowl

Ingredients:

For the Mexican Rice:

- 1 cup long-grain white rice
- 1 tablespoon vegetable oil
- 1 small onion, finely chopped
- 2 cloves garlic, minced
- 1 jalapeño, seeded and finely chopped (optional)
- 1 can (14 oz) diced tomatoes
- 1 teaspoon ground cumin
- 1 teaspoon chili powder
- 1/2 teaspoon paprika
- Salt and pepper, to taste
- 2 cups vegetable broth or water

For the Bowl:

- Cooked Mexican rice (from above)
- 1 can (15 oz) black beans, drained and rinsed
- Grilled or roasted vegetables (e.g., bell peppers, zucchini, corn)
- Sautéed fajita-style peppers and onions
- Sliced avocado or guacamole
- Salsa or pico de gallo
- Shredded lettuce or cabbage
- Chopped fresh cilantro
- Lime wedges
- Optional toppings: shredded cheese, sour cream or vegan sour cream

Instructions:

1. Prepare the Mexican Rice:

   1. Rinse the rice under cold water until the water runs clear.
   2. In a large skillet or pot, heat the vegetable oil over medium heat. Add the chopped onion and cook until translucent, about 3-4 minutes.
   3. Add the minced garlic and jalapeño (if using), and cook for another 1-2 minutes until fragrant.

4. Stir in the diced tomatoes (with their juices), ground cumin, chili powder, paprika, salt, and pepper. Cook for 2-3 minutes.
5. Add the rice to the skillet and stir to coat it with the tomato mixture.
6. Pour in the vegetable broth or water. Bring to a simmer, then reduce the heat to low. Cover and cook for 15-20 minutes, or until the rice is tender and the liquid is absorbed. Fluff the rice with a fork.

2. Assemble the Mexican Rice Bowl:

    1. Spoon a generous portion of the cooked Mexican rice into serving bowls.
    2. Top the rice with black beans, grilled or roasted vegetables, and sautéed peppers and onions.
    3. Add slices of avocado or guacamole, salsa or pico de gallo, shredded lettuce or cabbage, and chopped cilantro.
    4. Serve the rice bowls with lime wedges on the side for squeezing over the toppings.

3. Serve and Enjoy:

    - Serve the Mexican Rice Bowls immediately, allowing everyone to customize their bowls with their favorite toppings.
    - Feel free to add protein options such as grilled chicken, shrimp, tofu, or tempeh to make the bowls more substantial.

This Mexican Rice Bowl is a colorful and flavorful meal that's perfect for a quick and satisfying lunch or dinner. It's also great for meal prep, as you can prepare the components ahead of time and assemble when ready to eat. Enjoy the vibrant flavors of Mexican cuisine in this delicious rice bowl!

Falafel Bowl

Ingredients:

For the Falafel:

- 1 can (15 oz) chickpeas, drained and rinsed
- 1/2 cup chopped fresh parsley
- 1/2 cup chopped fresh cilantro
- 3 cloves garlic, minced
- 1 small onion, chopped
- 2 tablespoons all-purpose flour or chickpea flour (for gluten-free)
- 1 teaspoon ground cumin
- 1 teaspoon ground coriander
- 1/2 teaspoon baking powder
- Salt and pepper, to taste
- Vegetable oil, for frying

For the Bowl:

- Cooked quinoa, rice, or couscous
- Mixed greens or shredded lettuce
- Sliced cucumbers
- Sliced tomatoes
- Sliced red onions
- Kalamata olives
- Hummus
- Tzatziki sauce or tahini sauce
- Lemon wedges
- Fresh parsley or cilantro, for garnish

Instructions:

1. Prepare the Falafel:

   1. In a food processor, combine the chickpeas, parsley, cilantro, garlic, onion, flour, cumin, coriander, baking powder, salt, and pepper.
   2. Pulse until the mixture becomes a coarse paste, scraping down the sides of the processor as needed.
   3. Transfer the mixture to a bowl and refrigerate for 30 minutes to 1 hour to firm up.
   4. Shape the falafel mixture into small balls or patties.

2. Cook the Falafel:

    1. Heat vegetable oil in a skillet over medium heat.
    2. Fry the falafel in batches until golden brown and crispy, about 3-4 minutes per side. Drain on paper towels.

3. Assemble the Falafel Bowl:

    1. Start with a base of cooked quinoa, rice, or couscous in each serving bowl.
    2. Arrange mixed greens or shredded lettuce around the bowl.
    3. Top with sliced cucumbers, tomatoes, red onions, and Kalamata olives.
    4. Add several crispy falafel patties to each bowl.

4. Add Sauces and Garnishes:

    1. Spoon hummus and tzatziki sauce or tahini sauce over the falafel and vegetables.
    2. Garnish with fresh parsley or cilantro.
    3. Serve the Falafel Bowls with lemon wedges on the side for squeezing over the bowl before eating.

5. Serve and Enjoy:

    - Serve the Falafel Bowls immediately, allowing everyone to mix the ingredients and sauces together as they like.
    - Customize the bowls with additional toppings such as feta cheese, pickled vegetables, or hot sauce for extra flavor.

This Falafel Bowl is a satisfying and nutritious meal that's perfect for lunch or dinner. It's packed with protein, fiber, and a variety of fresh flavors. Enjoy the crispy falafel paired with creamy sauces and crunchy vegetables for a delightful culinary experience!

Sweet Potato and Kale Bowl

Ingredients:

For the Bowl:

- 2 medium sweet potatoes, peeled and cubed
- 1 tablespoon olive oil
- Salt and pepper, to taste
- 1 bunch kale, stems removed and leaves chopped
- 2 cloves garlic, minced
- Cooked quinoa or brown rice
- Sliced avocado
- Cooked chickpeas or black beans
- Toasted pumpkin seeds or nuts (e.g., almonds, pecans)
- Crumbled feta cheese or vegan cheese (optional)
- Lemon wedges, for serving

For the Dressing (optional):

- 3 tablespoons olive oil
- 1 tablespoon apple cider vinegar or lemon juice
- 1 tablespoon maple syrup or honey (substitute with agave syrup for vegan)
- 1 teaspoon Dijon mustard
- Salt and pepper, to taste

Instructions:

1. Roast the Sweet Potatoes:

    1. Preheat the oven to 400°F (200°C).
    2. Toss the cubed sweet potatoes with olive oil, salt, and pepper on a baking sheet.
    3. Roast in the preheated oven for 20-25 minutes or until tender and lightly caramelized. Flip halfway through cooking.

2. Sauté the Kale:

    1. In a large skillet, heat a little olive oil over medium heat.
    2. Add minced garlic and sauté for about 1 minute until fragrant.
    3. Add chopped kale to the skillet and sauté for 3-5 minutes until wilted but still vibrant green. Season with salt and pepper to taste.

3. Prepare the Dressing (optional):

    1. In a small bowl, whisk together olive oil, apple cider vinegar or lemon juice, maple syrup or honey, Dijon mustard, salt, and pepper. Adjust seasoning to taste.

4. Assemble the Sweet Potato and Kale Bowl:

    1. Divide cooked quinoa or brown rice among serving bowls.
    2. Top with roasted sweet potatoes, sautéed kale, sliced avocado, cooked chickpeas or black beans, and toasted pumpkin seeds or nuts.
    3. Drizzle with the optional dressing (if using) or serve with lemon wedges on the side.
    4. Optionally, sprinkle with crumbled feta cheese or vegan cheese for added flavor.

5. Serve and Enjoy:

    - Serve the Sweet Potato and Kale Bowls immediately, allowing everyone to mix the ingredients together and enjoy the flavors.
    - Feel free to customize the toppings based on your preferences, adding other vegetables, grains, or protein sources.

This Sweet Potato and Kale Bowl is a nutritious and filling meal that's perfect for a healthy lunch or dinner. It's packed with vitamins, fiber, and plant-based protein, making it a satisfying and wholesome dish. Enjoy the combination of roasted sweet potatoes, sautéed kale, and other delicious toppings in this vibrant bowl!

Coconut Curry Bowl

Ingredients:

For the Coconut Curry Sauce:

- 1 tablespoon vegetable oil
- 1 onion, finely chopped
- 3 cloves garlic, minced
- 1 tablespoon grated ginger
- 2 tablespoons red curry paste
- 1 can (14 oz) coconut milk
- 1 tablespoon soy sauce or tamari (for gluten-free)
- 1 tablespoon brown sugar or maple syrup
- Juice of 1 lime
- Salt and pepper, to taste

For the Bowl:

- Cooked rice or noodles of your choice
- Assorted vegetables (e.g., bell peppers, broccoli, carrots, snap peas)
- Protein of your choice (e.g., tofu, chickpeas, shrimp, chicken)
- Fresh cilantro, chopped
- Lime wedges, for serving
- Optional toppings: chopped peanuts, sliced green onions, chili flakes

Instructions:

1. Prepare the Coconut Curry Sauce:

    1. Heat vegetable oil in a large skillet or pot over medium heat.
    2. Add chopped onion, minced garlic, and grated ginger. Sauté until onion is translucent and aromatic, about 3-4 minutes.
    3. Stir in the red curry paste and cook for another 1-2 minutes until fragrant.
    4. Pour in the coconut milk, soy sauce (or tamari), and brown sugar (or maple syrup). Stir well to combine.
    5. Simmer the sauce gently for 5-7 minutes, stirring occasionally, until slightly thickened.
    6. Add lime juice, salt, and pepper to taste. Adjust seasoning as needed.

2. Cook the Vegetables and Protein:

1. While the sauce is simmering, prepare your vegetables and protein.
2. In a separate skillet, stir-fry or sauté your choice of vegetables until crisp-tender. Set aside.
3. Cook your protein (e.g., tofu, chickpeas, shrimp, chicken) according to your preference.

3. Assemble the Coconut Curry Bowl:

1. Divide cooked rice or noodles among serving bowls.
2. Ladle the coconut curry sauce over the rice or noodles.
3. Arrange the sautéed vegetables and cooked protein on top of the sauce.
4. Garnish with chopped fresh cilantro and serve with lime wedges on the side.

4. Add Optional Toppings:

1. Sprinkle chopped peanuts, sliced green onions, or chili flakes over the Coconut Curry Bowl for added texture and flavor.

5. Serve and Enjoy:

- Serve the Coconut Curry Bowl immediately, allowing everyone to mix the ingredients together and squeeze fresh lime juice over their bowls.
- Enjoy the rich and aromatic flavors of the coconut curry sauce paired with tender vegetables and protein.

This Coconut Curry Bowl is a versatile and comforting meal that's perfect for a weeknight dinner or a casual gathering. Customize the bowl with your favorite vegetables and protein to make it your own. It's sure to be a hit with family and friends!

Sushi Bowl

Ingredients:

For the Sushi Rice:

- 1 cup sushi rice (short-grain Japanese rice)
- 1 1/4 cups water
- 2 tablespoons rice vinegar
- 1 tablespoon sugar
- 1/2 teaspoon salt

For the Sushi Bowl:

- Sushi rice (prepared from the above ingredients)
- Sushi-grade fish (e.g., salmon, tuna, or cooked options like shrimp or crab)
- Sliced avocado
- Sliced cucumber
- Shredded nori (seaweed sheets)
- Pickled ginger (optional)
- Soy sauce or tamari, for drizzling
- Wasabi (optional)

Instructions:

1. Prepare the Sushi Rice:

    1. Rinse the sushi rice under cold water until the water runs clear. Drain well.
    2. In a rice cooker or a pot, combine the rice and water. Cook the rice according to the manufacturer's instructions (usually 1:1 ratio of rice to water).
    3. While the rice is cooking, prepare the sushi vinegar mixture. In a small bowl, mix rice vinegar, sugar, and salt until dissolved.
    4. Once the rice is cooked, transfer it to a large bowl. Gradually add the sushi vinegar mixture to the rice, folding gently with a rice paddle or spatula to combine. Let the rice cool slightly.

2. Assemble the Sushi Bowl:

    1. Divide the sushi rice among serving bowls.
    2. Arrange slices of sushi-grade fish (or cooked protein) on top of the rice.
    3. Add sliced avocado, sliced cucumber, and shredded nori to the bowls.
    4. Garnish with pickled ginger if desired.

3. Serve and Enjoy:

- Drizzle soy sauce or tamari over the sushi bowl.
- Optionally, serve with wasabi on the side for extra heat.
- Mix the ingredients together in the bowl before eating to combine the flavors.

Tips for Customization:

- Variety of Proteins: Aside from sushi-grade fish, you can use cooked shrimp, crab meat, or tofu as protein options.
- Vegetarian/Vegan Options: Replace fish with marinated tofu, tempura vegetables, or pickled vegetables for a vegetarian or vegan version.
- Additional Toppings: Customize with other toppings like radishes, edamame beans, tobiko (flying fish roe), or sesame seeds.
- Sauce Options: Drizzle with spicy mayo, eel sauce, or ponzu sauce for extra flavor.

This Sushi Bowl recipe offers a convenient way to enjoy the flavors of sushi without the need for rolling or shaping sushi rolls. It's perfect for a quick lunch or dinner and can be easily customized based on your preferences. Enjoy the fresh and vibrant taste of sushi in this delicious bowl format!

Moroccan Couscous Bowl

Ingredients:

For the Couscous:

- 1 cup couscous
- 1 1/4 cups vegetable broth or water
- 1 tablespoon olive oil
- Salt, to taste

For the Moroccan Spice Blend:

- 1 teaspoon ground cumin
- 1 teaspoon ground coriander
- 1/2 teaspoon ground cinnamon
- 1/2 teaspoon ground turmeric
- 1/2 teaspoon paprika
- 1/4 teaspoon cayenne pepper (adjust to taste)
- Salt and pepper, to taste

For the Bowl:

- 1 tablespoon olive oil
- 1 onion, finely chopped
- 2 cloves garlic, minced
- 1 bell pepper, diced
- 1 zucchini, diced
- 1 carrot, diced
- 1 can (15 oz) chickpeas, drained and rinsed
- 1/2 cup dried apricots, chopped
- 1/4 cup golden raisins
- 1/4 cup sliced almonds, toasted
- Fresh parsley or cilantro, chopped (for garnish)
- Lemon wedges, for serving

Instructions:

1. Prepare the Couscous:
   1. In a saucepan, bring the vegetable broth or water to a boil.

2. Stir in the couscous, olive oil, and a pinch of salt. Remove from heat, cover, and let sit for about 5 minutes until the couscous has absorbed the liquid. Fluff with a fork.

2. Make the Moroccan Spice Blend:

    1. In a small bowl, combine the ground cumin, coriander, cinnamon, turmeric, paprika, cayenne pepper, salt, and pepper. Set aside.

3. Prepare the Bowl:

    1. Heat olive oil in a large skillet over medium heat.
    2. Add the chopped onion and sauté until translucent, about 3-4 minutes.
    3. Stir in the minced garlic and Moroccan spice blend. Cook for another minute until fragrant.
    4. Add the diced bell pepper, zucchini, and carrot to the skillet. Sauté for 5-7 minutes until the vegetables start to soften.
    5. Stir in the drained chickpeas, chopped dried apricots, and golden raisins. Cook for another 2-3 minutes to heat through.
    6. Add the cooked couscous to the skillet with the vegetables and chickpeas. Mix well to combine and heat everything together.
    7. Taste and adjust seasoning as needed with salt and pepper.

4. Serve the Moroccan Couscous Bowl:

    1. Divide the Moroccan couscous mixture among serving bowls.
    2. Top each bowl with toasted sliced almonds and chopped fresh parsley or cilantro.
    3. Serve with lemon wedges on the side for squeezing over the bowl before eating.

5. Enjoy!

    - Serve the Moroccan Couscous Bowl immediately, allowing everyone to enjoy the blend of flavors and textures.
    - Feel free to customize the bowl with additional toppings like feta cheese, diced tomatoes, or a dollop of Greek yogurt for extra creaminess.

This Moroccan Couscous Bowl is a delightful meal that's packed with Moroccan-inspired spices, sweet dried fruits, and nutritious vegetables. It's perfect for a wholesome lunch or dinner that's full of flavor and satisfying textures. Enjoy the taste of Morocco with this delicious couscous bowl!

Greek Salad Bowl

Ingredients:

For the Salad:

- 2 cups cherry tomatoes, halved
- 1 cucumber, diced
- 1 bell pepper (any color), diced
- 1/2 red onion, thinly sliced
- 1/2 cup Kalamata olives, pitted
- 1/2 cup crumbled feta cheese
- 1/4 cup chopped fresh parsley
- Optional: 1/4 cup thinly sliced red cabbage for color

For the Dressing:

- 1/4 cup extra-virgin olive oil
- 2 tablespoons red wine vinegar
- 1 tablespoon freshly squeezed lemon juice
- 1 clove garlic, minced
- 1 teaspoon dried oregano
- Salt and pepper, to taste

For Serving:

- Cooked quinoa, couscous, or rice
- Grilled chicken, shrimp, or tofu (optional)
- Lemon wedges, for serving
- Additional fresh parsley or oregano, for garnish

Instructions:

1. Prepare the Salad Ingredients:

   1. In a large mixing bowl, combine the halved cherry tomatoes, diced cucumber, diced bell pepper, thinly sliced red onion, pitted Kalamata olives, crumbled feta cheese, chopped fresh parsley, and red cabbage (if using). Toss gently to combine.

2. Make the Dressing:

1. In a small bowl or jar, whisk together the extra-virgin olive oil, red wine vinegar, freshly squeezed lemon juice, minced garlic, dried oregano, salt, and pepper until well combined.

3. Assemble the Greek Salad Bowl:
   1. Divide cooked quinoa, couscous, or rice among serving bowls.
   2. Spoon the prepared Greek salad mixture over the grains in each bowl.
   3. If adding protein, such as grilled chicken, shrimp, or tofu, arrange it on top of the salad.

4. Serve and Enjoy:
   1. Drizzle the Greek salad dressing over each salad bowl.
   2. Garnish with additional fresh parsley or oregano.
   3. Serve with lemon wedges on the side for squeezing over the salad before eating.

5. Tips for Serving:
   - For a vegetarian or vegan version, omit the feta cheese or use a dairy-free alternative.
   - Customize the salad with additional toppings like sliced avocado, roasted red peppers, or capers.
   - Serve the Greek Salad Bowl as a main dish for lunch or dinner, or as a side salad alongside grilled meats or seafood.

This Greek Salad Bowl is a delicious and healthy meal that's perfect for a light and satisfying lunch or dinner. Enjoy the classic Mediterranean flavors of tomatoes, cucumbers, olives, and feta cheese in this vibrant salad bowl!

Avocado and Black Bean Bowl

Ingredients:

For the Bowl:

- 1 cup cooked quinoa or brown rice
- 1 can (15 oz) black beans, drained and rinsed
- 1 avocado, sliced
- 1 cup cherry tomatoes, halved
- 1/2 cup corn kernels (fresh or canned)
- 1/4 cup diced red onion
- 1/4 cup chopped fresh cilantro
- Lime wedges, for serving

For the Dressing:

- 2 tablespoons olive oil
- 2 tablespoons lime juice
- 1 clove garlic, minced
- 1 teaspoon ground cumin
- Salt and pepper, to taste

Optional Toppings:

- Sliced jalapeños (for spice)
- Sliced bell peppers
- Shredded lettuce or spinach
- Sliced radishes
- Crumbled feta cheese or cotija cheese (for non-vegan option)
- Tortilla chips or strips

Instructions:

1. Prepare the Dressing:
    1. In a small bowl, whisk together olive oil, lime juice, minced garlic, ground cumin, salt, and pepper. Set aside.

2. Assemble the Bowl:
    1. Divide cooked quinoa or brown rice among serving bowls.

2. Arrange black beans, sliced avocado, cherry tomatoes, corn kernels, diced red onion, and chopped cilantro on top of the quinoa or rice.

3. Drizzle with Dressing:

   1. Drizzle the prepared dressing over each bowl.

4. Add Optional Toppings:

   1. Customize the bowls with optional toppings such as sliced jalapeños, bell peppers, shredded lettuce or spinach, sliced radishes, and crumbled feta or cotija cheese (if using).
   2. Serve with lime wedges on the side for squeezing over the bowl.

5. Serve and Enjoy:

   - Toss the ingredients together before eating to combine the flavors.
   - Optionally, serve the Avocado and Black Bean Bowl with tortilla chips or strips for added crunch.

Tips:

- Protein Options: Add grilled chicken, shrimp, or tofu for additional protein.
- Make It Spicy: Increase the heat by adding more jalapeños or a dash of hot sauce.
- Meal Prep: This bowl is great for meal prep. Prepare the components ahead of time and assemble when ready to eat.

This Avocado and Black Bean Bowl is a nutritious and flavorful meal that's perfect for a quick and satisfying lunch or dinner. It's loaded with healthy ingredients and can be easily customized based on your preferences. Enjoy the creamy avocado, hearty black beans, and zesty dressing in this delicious bowl!

Roasted Veggie Quinoa Bowl

Ingredients:

For the Roasted Vegetables:

- 2 cups mixed vegetables (such as bell peppers, zucchini, broccoli, cauliflower, cherry tomatoes)
- 2 tablespoons olive oil
- 1 teaspoon dried herbs (such as thyme, rosemary, or Italian seasoning)
- Salt and pepper, to taste

For the Quinoa:

- 1 cup quinoa, rinsed
- 2 cups vegetable broth or water
- Salt, to taste

For the Bowl Assembly:

- Cooked quinoa (from above)
- Roasted vegetables (from above)
- 1 avocado, sliced
- 1/4 cup crumbled feta cheese or goat cheese (optional)
- Fresh herbs (such as parsley or basil), chopped
- Lemon wedges, for serving
- Optional dressing (e.g., balsamic vinaigrette, tahini dressing, or lemon-garlic dressing)

Instructions:

1. Roast the Vegetables:
    1. Preheat the oven to 400°F (200°C).
    2. Chop the vegetables into bite-sized pieces and place them on a baking sheet.
    3. Drizzle with olive oil, sprinkle with dried herbs, salt, and pepper. Toss to coat evenly.
    4. Roast in the preheated oven for 20-25 minutes, or until the vegetables are tender and slightly caramelized. Stir halfway through cooking.

2. Cook the Quinoa:
    1. Rinse the quinoa under cold water using a fine mesh sieve.

2. In a saucepan, combine the rinsed quinoa and vegetable broth or water. Bring to a boil.
3. Reduce the heat to low, cover, and simmer for 15-20 minutes, or until the quinoa is cooked and the liquid is absorbed. Fluff with a fork and season with salt to taste.

3. Assemble the Bowl:

   1. Divide the cooked quinoa among serving bowls.
   2. Top with the roasted vegetables.
   3. Add sliced avocado, crumbled feta or goat cheese (if using), and chopped fresh herbs on top.

4. Serve and Enjoy:

   - Serve the Roasted Veggie Quinoa Bowl with lemon wedges on the side for squeezing over the bowl.
   - Drizzle with your favorite dressing, if desired, or enjoy as is for a lighter option.

Tips:

- Protein Boost: Add grilled chicken, tofu, chickpeas, or sliced hard-boiled eggs for additional protein.
- Variety of Vegetables: Feel free to use any seasonal vegetables you like for roasting.
- Make It Vegan: Omit the cheese or use a dairy-free alternative to keep the bowl vegan-friendly.
- Meal Prep: This bowl is great for meal prep. Prepare the quinoa and roast the vegetables ahead of time, then assemble the bowls when ready to eat.

This Roasted Veggie Quinoa Bowl is a nutritious and versatile meal that's perfect for lunch or dinner. It's packed with fiber, vitamins, and minerals from the vegetables and quinoa, making it a satisfying and wholesome dish. Enjoy the delicious flavors and textures in this easy-to-make bowl!

Lemon Herb Tempeh Bowl

Ingredients:

For the Lemon Herb Tempeh:

- 1 package (8 oz) tempeh, sliced into strips or cubes
- Zest and juice of 1 lemon
- 2 tablespoons olive oil
- 2 cloves garlic, minced
- 1 tablespoon chopped fresh herbs (such as parsley, thyme, or rosemary)
- Salt and pepper, to taste

For the Bowl:

- Cooked quinoa, brown rice, or farro
- Mixed salad greens or spinach
- Sliced cucumber
- Cherry tomatoes, halved
- Sliced radishes
- Sliced avocado
- Optional toppings: toasted nuts or seeds, crumbled feta cheese or vegan cheese

For the Dressing:

- 3 tablespoons extra-virgin olive oil
- 2 tablespoons lemon juice
- 1 tablespoon Dijon mustard
- 1 teaspoon honey or maple syrup (substitute with agave syrup for vegan)
- Salt and pepper, to taste

Instructions:

1. Marinate the Tempeh:
    1. In a shallow dish or bowl, combine lemon zest, lemon juice, olive oil, minced garlic, chopped fresh herbs, salt, and pepper.
    2. Add the tempeh slices or cubes to the marinade, tossing gently to coat. Allow the tempeh to marinate for at least 30 minutes, or ideally up to 2 hours in the refrigerator.

2. Cook the Tempeh:

1. Heat a non-stick skillet or grill pan over medium heat.
2. Add the marinated tempeh to the skillet, reserving the marinade.
3. Cook the tempeh for 3-4 minutes on each side, or until golden brown and slightly crispy. Use a brush to baste the tempeh with the remaining marinade while cooking.

3. Prepare the Dressing:

    1. In a small bowl, whisk together extra-virgin olive oil, lemon juice, Dijon mustard, honey or maple syrup, salt, and pepper until well combined. Adjust seasoning to taste.

4. Assemble the Lemon Herb Tempeh Bowl:

    1. Divide cooked quinoa, brown rice, or farro among serving bowls.
    2. Arrange mixed salad greens or spinach, sliced cucumber, cherry tomatoes, sliced radishes, and sliced avocado on top of the grains.
    3. Place the cooked lemon herb tempeh on top of the salad.

5. Drizzle with Dressing and Add Toppings:

    1. Drizzle the prepared dressing over each bowl.
    2. Sprinkle with optional toppings such as toasted nuts or seeds, crumbled feta cheese or vegan cheese.

6. Serve and Enjoy:

    - Serve the Lemon Herb Tempeh Bowl immediately, allowing everyone to mix the ingredients together and enjoy the flavors.
    - Customize the bowl with additional toppings or vegetables based on your preferences.

Tips:

- **Meal Prep:** You can marinate the tempeh ahead of time and cook it when ready to assemble the bowls.
- **Protein Options:** Substitute tempeh with grilled chicken, tofu, or chickpeas for a different variation.
- **Make It Vegan:** Use maple syrup instead of honey in the dressing, and omit the cheese or use a vegan alternative for a vegan-friendly bowl.

This Lemon Herb Tempeh Bowl is a delightful combination of flavors and textures, perfect for a nutritious and satisfying meal. Enjoy the tangy and savory tempeh paired with fresh vegetables and grains in this delicious bowl!

Vegan Bibimbap Bowl

Ingredients:

For the Rice:

- 1 cup uncooked short-grain rice
- 2 cups water
- Pinch of salt

For the Vegetables:

- 1 tablespoon sesame oil
- 1 block (14 oz) firm tofu, pressed and cut into cubes
- 2 cups sliced mixed vegetables (such as carrots, zucchini, bell peppers, spinach, mushrooms)
- Salt, to taste

For the Bibimbap Sauce:

- 3 tablespoons gochujang (Korean chili paste)
- 1 tablespoon soy sauce or tamari (for gluten-free)
- 1 tablespoon sesame oil
- 1 tablespoon maple syrup or sugar
- 2 cloves garlic, minced
- 1 tablespoon rice vinegar

For Serving:

- Kimchi (optional)
- Fresh lettuce or spinach leaves
- Sesame seeds, for garnish
- Thinly sliced green onions, for garnish

Instructions:

1. Cook the Rice:

   1. Rinse the rice under cold water until the water runs clear.
   2. In a rice cooker or pot, combine the rinsed rice, water, and a pinch of salt. Cook the rice according to the manufacturer's instructions.

2. Prepare the Tofu and Vegetables:

1. Heat sesame oil in a large skillet over medium-high heat.
2. Add the tofu cubes and cook until golden and crispy on all sides. Remove the tofu from the skillet and set aside.
3. In the same skillet, add more sesame oil if needed and stir-fry the mixed vegetables until tender-crisp. Season with salt to taste.

3. Make the Bibimbap Sauce:

1. In a small bowl, whisk together gochujang, soy sauce or tamari, sesame oil, maple syrup or sugar, minced garlic, and rice vinegar until well combined. Adjust seasoning to taste.

4. Assemble the Vegan Bibimbap Bowl:

1. Divide the cooked rice among serving bowls.
2. Arrange the cooked tofu and stir-fried vegetables on top of the rice.
3. Add a spoonful of bibimbap sauce on the side or drizzle it over the tofu and vegetables.
4. Serve with fresh lettuce or spinach leaves on the side.

5. Garnish and Serve:

1. Garnish the bowls with kimchi (if using), sesame seeds, and thinly sliced green onions.
2. Mix everything together before eating to combine the flavors and textures.

Tips:

- Variation: Feel free to add other toppings such as sautéed shiitake mushrooms, sliced cucumbers, or bean sprouts.
- Spice Level: Adjust the amount of gochujang to your preferred spice level.
- Meal Prep: Prepare the rice, tofu, and vegetables ahead of time and assemble the bowls when ready to eat.
- Gluten-Free Option: Use tamari instead of soy sauce to make the dish gluten-free.

This Vegan Bibimbap Bowl is a delicious and satisfying meal that's packed with flavors and nutrients. Enjoy the combination of crispy tofu, vibrant vegetables, and spicy bibimbap sauce over fluffy rice for a delightful Korean-inspired dish!

Butternut Squash Buddha Bowl

Ingredients:

For the Roasted Butternut Squash:

- 1 small butternut squash, peeled, seeded, and cut into cubes
- 2 tablespoons olive oil
- 1 tablespoon maple syrup
- 1/2 teaspoon ground cinnamon
- Salt and pepper, to taste

For the Bowl:

- Cooked quinoa, brown rice, or farro
- Mixed salad greens or spinach
- 1 can (15 oz) chickpeas, drained and rinsed
- 1 avocado, sliced
- 1/4 cup pumpkin seeds or chopped nuts (e.g., pecans, walnuts)
- Optional: crumbled feta cheese or goat cheese (omit for vegan)

For the Dressing:

- 3 tablespoons extra-virgin olive oil
- 2 tablespoons apple cider vinegar
- 1 tablespoon maple syrup
- 1 teaspoon Dijon mustard
- Salt and pepper, to taste

Instructions:

1. Roast the Butternut Squash:

   1. Preheat the oven to 400°F (200°C).
   2. In a bowl, toss the cubed butternut squash with olive oil, maple syrup, ground cinnamon, salt, and pepper until well coated.
   3. Spread the squash on a baking sheet in a single layer.
   4. Roast in the preheated oven for 25-30 minutes, or until the squash is tender and caramelized, flipping halfway through cooking.

2. Prepare the Dressing:

1. In a small bowl, whisk together extra-virgin olive oil, apple cider vinegar, maple syrup, Dijon mustard, salt, and pepper until well combined. Set aside.

3. Assemble the Butternut Squash Buddha Bowl:
    1. Divide cooked quinoa, brown rice, or farro among serving bowls.
    2. Arrange mixed salad greens or spinach on one side of the bowl.
    3. On the other side of the bowl, arrange the roasted butternut squash, chickpeas, sliced avocado, and pumpkin seeds or chopped nuts.
    4. If using, sprinkle crumbled feta cheese or goat cheese over the bowl.

4. Drizzle with Dressing and Serve:
    1. Drizzle the prepared dressing over each Butternut Squash Buddha Bowl.
    2. Serve immediately and enjoy!

Tips:

- Protein Options: Add grilled tofu, tempeh, or sliced chicken for additional protein.
- Variations: Feel free to add other vegetables such as roasted Brussels sprouts, broccoli, or cauliflower.
- Make It Vegan: Omit the cheese or use a vegan cheese alternative.
- Meal Prep: Prepare the components ahead of time and assemble the bowls when ready to eat.

This Butternut Squash Buddha Bowl is a satisfying and nourishing meal that's perfect for a healthy lunch or dinner. Enjoy the sweetness of roasted butternut squash paired with grains, greens, and protein in this delicious bowl!

Edamame and Brown Rice Bowl

Ingredients:

For the Bowl:

- 1 cup cooked brown rice
- 1 cup shelled edamame (fresh or frozen)
- 1 carrot, grated
- 1 cucumber, diced
- 1 avocado, sliced
- 2 green onions, thinly sliced
- Sesame seeds, for garnish
- Optional: sliced radishes, shredded cabbage, microgreens

For the Dressing:

- 2 tablespoons soy sauce or tamari (for gluten-free)
- 1 tablespoon rice vinegar
- 1 tablespoon sesame oil
- 1 tablespoon honey or maple syrup (substitute with agave syrup for vegan)
- 1 clove garlic, minced
- 1 teaspoon grated ginger
- Red pepper flakes, to taste (optional)

Instructions:

1. Cook the Brown Rice:
    1. Cook brown rice according to package instructions until tender. Set aside.

2. Prepare the Edamame:
    1. If using frozen edamame, cook according to package instructions. Drain and set aside.

3. Make the Dressing:
    1. In a small bowl, whisk together soy sauce or tamari, rice vinegar, sesame oil, honey or maple syrup, minced garlic, grated ginger, and red pepper flakes (if using). Set aside.

4. Assemble the Edamame and Brown Rice Bowl:

1. Divide cooked brown rice among serving bowls.
2. Arrange cooked edamame, grated carrot, diced cucumber, sliced avocado, and green onions on top of the rice.
3. Drizzle the dressing over the bowl.

5. Garnish and Serve:

1. Sprinkle sesame seeds and any optional toppings (such as sliced radishes, shredded cabbage, or microgreens) over the bowl.
2. Serve immediately and enjoy!

Tips:

- Protein Boost: Add grilled tofu, tempeh, or chickpeas for additional protein.
- Variations: Customize with your favorite vegetables such as bell peppers, spinach, or cherry tomatoes.
- Make It Vegan: Use maple syrup instead of honey in the dressing, and ensure all ingredients are vegan-friendly.
- Meal Prep: Prepare the components ahead of time and assemble the bowls when ready to eat.

This Edamame and Brown Rice Bowl is a delicious and wholesome meal that's packed with nutrients and flavor. Enjoy the combination of chewy brown rice, tender edamame, creamy avocado, and crunchy vegetables in this delightful bowl!

Chickpea Shawarma Bowl

Ingredients:

For the Chickpea Shawarma:

- 1 can (15 oz) chickpeas, drained and rinsed
- 2 tablespoons olive oil
- 2 teaspoons ground cumin
- 1 teaspoon paprika
- 1/2 teaspoon ground turmeric
- 1/2 teaspoon ground cinnamon
- Salt and pepper, to taste

For the Bowl:

- Cooked quinoa or rice
- Mixed salad greens or shredded lettuce
- Sliced cucumber
- Cherry tomatoes, halved
- Sliced red onion
- Sliced avocado
- Fresh parsley or cilantro, chopped
- Lemon wedges, for serving

For the Tahini Dressing:

- 1/4 cup tahini
- 2 tablespoons water
- 2 tablespoons lemon juice
- 1 clove garlic, minced
- Salt and pepper, to taste

Instructions:

1. Prepare the Chickpea Shawarma:
    1. Preheat the oven to 400°F (200°C).
    2. In a bowl, combine the drained chickpeas with olive oil, ground cumin, paprika, turmeric, cinnamon, salt, and pepper. Toss until the chickpeas are well coated.
    3. Spread the seasoned chickpeas on a baking sheet in a single layer.

4. Roast in the preheated oven for 20-25 minutes, or until the chickpeas are crispy and golden brown.

2. Make the Tahini Dressing:

1. In a small bowl, whisk together tahini, water, lemon juice, minced garlic, salt, and pepper until smooth and creamy. Add more water if needed to reach desired consistency.

3. Assemble the Chickpea Shawarma Bowl:

1. Divide cooked quinoa or rice among serving bowls.
2. Arrange mixed salad greens or shredded lettuce, sliced cucumber, halved cherry tomatoes, sliced red onion, sliced avocado, and roasted chickpeas on top of the quinoa or rice.
3. Drizzle the tahini dressing over the bowl.
4. Garnish with chopped fresh parsley or cilantro.
5. Serve with lemon wedges on the side for squeezing over the bowl before eating.

4. Enjoy!

- Mix the ingredients together in the bowl before eating to combine the flavors.
- Adjust seasoning and add more dressing or lemon juice, if desired.

Tips:

- Protein Options: Add grilled chicken, tofu, or falafel for additional protein.
- Variations: Customize with your favorite vegetables such as bell peppers, shredded carrots, or olives.
- Make It Vegan: Ensure all ingredients used are vegan-friendly, including the dressing.
- Meal Prep: Prepare the components ahead of time and assemble the bowls when ready to eat.

This Chickpea Shawarma Bowl is a flavorful and nutritious meal that's perfect for lunch or dinner. Enjoy the aromatic spices of the chickpeas paired with fresh vegetables and creamy tahini dressing in this delicious bowl!

Vegan Caesar Salad Bowl

Ingredients:

For the Vegan Caesar Dressing:

- 1/2 cup raw cashews, soaked in hot water for 1 hour (or overnight in cold water)
- 2 tablespoons lemon juice
- 1 tablespoon Dijon mustard
- 1 tablespoon capers
- 1 tablespoon nutritional yeast
- 1 clove garlic, minced
- 1/4 cup water (or more as needed to thin)
- Salt and pepper, to taste

For the Salad:

- 1 large head of romaine lettuce, chopped
- 1 cup cherry tomatoes, halved
- 1/2 cup cooked chickpeas (optional, for added protein)
- 1/4 cup sliced red onion
- 1/4 cup sliced cucumber
- Croutons (homemade or store-bought)
- Vegan Parmesan cheese (optional)

Instructions:

1. Make the Vegan Caesar Dressing:

    1. Drain and rinse the soaked cashews.
    2. In a blender or food processor, combine the soaked cashews, lemon juice, Dijon mustard, capers, nutritional yeast, minced garlic, water, salt, and pepper.
    3. Blend until smooth and creamy, adding more water as needed to reach desired consistency. Adjust seasoning to taste.

2. Assemble the Salad Bowl:

    1. In a large mixing bowl, combine chopped romaine lettuce, cherry tomatoes, cooked chickpeas (if using), sliced red onion, and sliced cucumber.
    2. Toss the salad ingredients with the prepared vegan Caesar dressing until well coated.

3. Serve the Vegan Caesar Salad Bowl:
   1. Divide the dressed salad among serving bowls.
   2. Top each bowl with croutons and vegan Parmesan cheese, if desired.
   3. Serve immediately and enjoy!

Tips:

- Croutons: To make homemade croutons, toss cubed bread with olive oil, garlic powder, and dried herbs (such as oregano or thyme). Bake in the oven at 375°F (190°C) for about 10-15 minutes, or until golden and crispy.
- Protein Options: Add grilled tofu, tempeh, or marinated chickpeas for extra protein.
- Variations: Customize the salad with your favorite vegetables or add avocado slices for creaminess.
- Make It Gluten-Free: Use gluten-free croutons or skip them altogether.
- Meal Prep: Prepare the dressing and salad ingredients ahead of time, but dress the salad just before serving to keep it fresh and crisp.

This Vegan Caesar Salad Bowl is a delicious and satisfying meal that's perfect for a quick lunch or dinner. Enjoy the creamy and tangy flavors of the homemade Caesar dressing paired with crisp romaine lettuce and tasty toppings!

Ratatouille Bowl

Ingredients:

For the Ratatouille:

- 2 tablespoons olive oil
- 1 onion, diced
- 3 cloves garlic, minced
- 1 eggplant, diced
- 2 zucchini, diced
- 1 bell pepper (any color), diced
- 2 cups diced tomatoes (fresh or canned)
- 1 tablespoon tomato paste
- 1 teaspoon dried thyme
- 1 teaspoon dried basil
- Salt and pepper, to taste

For the Bowl:

- Cooked quinoa, brown rice, or pasta
- Fresh basil leaves, chopped (for garnish)
- Grated Parmesan cheese or vegan cheese (optional)

Instructions:

1. Prepare the Ratatouille:

    1. Heat olive oil in a large skillet or pot over medium heat.
    2. Add diced onion and minced garlic. Sauté until softened and translucent, about 5 minutes.
    3. Add diced eggplant, zucchini, and bell pepper to the skillet. Cook for 8-10 minutes, stirring occasionally, until the vegetables start to soften.
    4. Stir in diced tomatoes, tomato paste, dried thyme, dried basil, salt, and pepper. Mix well to combine.
    5. Reduce heat to low, cover, and simmer for 20-25 minutes, stirring occasionally, until the vegetables are tender and the flavors have melded together. Adjust seasoning to taste.

2. Assemble the Ratatouille Bowl:

    1. Divide cooked quinoa, brown rice, or pasta among serving bowls.

2. Spoon the prepared ratatouille over the grains or pasta.

3. Garnish and Serve:
    1. Garnish each bowl with chopped fresh basil leaves.
    2. Optionally, sprinkle grated Parmesan cheese or vegan cheese on top for added flavor.

4. Enjoy!
   - Serve the Ratatouille Bowl immediately, allowing everyone to enjoy the rich flavors of the ratatouille over grains or pasta.

Tips:
- Variations: Customize the ratatouille by adding other vegetables like mushrooms or diced carrots.
- Protein Options: Add cooked chickpeas, lentils, or grilled tofu for added protein.
- Make It Vegan: Ensure the tomato paste and optional toppings are vegan-friendly.
- Meal Prep: Ratatouille can be made ahead of time and stored in the refrigerator. Reheat before serving over grains or pasta.

This Ratatouille Bowl is a comforting and satisfying meal that's perfect for showcasing the flavors of fresh vegetables and aromatic herbs. Enjoy this classic French dish in a convenient bowl format, topped with your favorite grains or pasta!

Buffalo Cauliflower Bowl

Ingredients:

For the Buffalo Cauliflower:

- 1 head of cauliflower, cut into florets
- 1/2 cup all-purpose flour (or chickpea flour for a gluten-free option)
- 1/2 cup water
- 1 teaspoon garlic powder
- 1 teaspoon onion powder
- Salt and pepper, to taste
- 1 cup buffalo hot sauce (or your favorite hot sauce)
- 2 tablespoons melted vegan butter or olive oil

For the Bowl:

- Cooked quinoa, brown rice, or cauliflower rice
- Mixed salad greens or spinach
- Sliced celery
- Sliced carrots
- Sliced red onion
- Vegan ranch dressing or tahini dressing

Instructions:

1. Prepare the Buffalo Cauliflower:
    1. Preheat the oven to 450°F (230°C) and line a baking sheet with parchment paper.
    2. In a bowl, whisk together flour, water, garlic powder, onion powder, salt, and pepper to make a batter.
    3. Dip each cauliflower floret into the batter, shaking off any excess, and place on the prepared baking sheet.
    4. Bake for 20-25 minutes, flipping halfway through, until the cauliflower is crispy and golden brown.

2. Make the Buffalo Sauce:
    1. In a separate bowl, mix together buffalo hot sauce and melted vegan butter or olive oil.
    2. Once the cauliflower is done baking, remove from the oven and toss in the buffalo sauce until evenly coated.

3. Assemble the Buffalo Cauliflower Bowl:

    1. Divide cooked quinoa, brown rice, or cauliflower rice among serving bowls.
    2. Arrange mixed salad greens or spinach, sliced celery, sliced carrots, and sliced red onion on top of the grains.
    3. Top with the crispy buffalo cauliflower.

4. Drizzle with Dressing and Serve:

    1. Drizzle vegan ranch dressing or tahini dressing over the bowl.
    2. Serve immediately and enjoy!

Tips:

- Spice Level: Adjust the amount of buffalo sauce to your preferred spice level.
- Protein Options: Add cooked chickpeas, black beans, or grilled tofu for additional protein.
- Variations: Customize the bowl with your favorite vegetables such as cherry tomatoes, bell peppers, or avocado slices.
- Make It Gluten-Free: Use chickpea flour instead of all-purpose flour for the batter, and ensure the buffalo sauce is gluten-free.

This Buffalo Cauliflower Bowl is a flavorful and satisfying meal that's perfect for a quick and tasty dinner. Enjoy the spicy kick of the buffalo cauliflower paired with fresh vegetables and creamy dressing in this delicious bowl!

Pesto Pasta Bowl

Ingredients:

For the Pesto Sauce:

- 2 cups fresh basil leaves, packed
- 1/2 cup pine nuts or walnuts
- 1/2 cup grated Parmesan cheese (or nutritional yeast for vegan option)
- 2 cloves garlic, minced
- 1/2 cup extra-virgin olive oil
- Salt and pepper, to taste

For the Pasta Bowl:

- 12 oz (340g) pasta of your choice (such as spaghetti, fettuccine, or penne)
- 1 cup cherry tomatoes, halved
- 1 cup baby spinach leaves
- 1/2 cup sliced black olives (optional)
- 1/4 cup sun-dried tomatoes, chopped (optional)
- Additional grated Parmesan cheese or vegan Parmesan (for topping)
- Fresh basil leaves, chopped (for garnish)

Instructions:

1. Prepare the Pesto Sauce:

    1. In a food processor or blender, combine fresh basil leaves, pine nuts or walnuts, grated Parmesan cheese (or nutritional yeast), minced garlic, salt, and pepper.
    2. Pulse until the ingredients are finely chopped.
    3. With the food processor running, slowly drizzle in the olive oil until the pesto reaches a smooth and creamy consistency. Adjust seasoning to taste.

2. Cook the Pasta:

    1. Bring a large pot of salted water to a boil.
    2. Cook the pasta according to package instructions until al dente. Drain and set aside, reserving a cup of pasta water.

3. Assemble the Pesto Pasta Bowl:

1. In a large mixing bowl, toss the cooked pasta with the prepared pesto sauce until well coated. If needed, add a splash of reserved pasta water to thin out the sauce.
2. Add cherry tomatoes, baby spinach leaves, sliced black olives (if using), and sun-dried tomatoes (if using) to the bowl. Toss to combine.
3. Divide the pesto pasta among serving bowls.

4. Garnish and Serve:

   1. Top each bowl with additional grated Parmesan cheese or vegan Parmesan.
   2. Garnish with chopped fresh basil leaves.
   3. Serve immediately and enjoy!

Tips:

- Variations: Customize the Pesto Pasta Bowl with your favorite vegetables such as roasted bell peppers, artichoke hearts, or sautéed mushrooms.
- Protein Options: Add grilled chicken, shrimp, tofu, or chickpeas for additional protein.
- Make It Vegan: Use nutritional yeast instead of Parmesan cheese in the pesto sauce, and ensure all other ingredients are vegan-friendly.
- Meal Prep: Prepare the pesto sauce and cook the pasta ahead of time, then assemble the bowls when ready to eat.

This Pesto Pasta Bowl is a comforting and flavorful meal that's perfect for a quick and easy dinner. Enjoy the vibrant green pesto paired with pasta and fresh vegetables in this delicious bowl!

Green Goddess Bowl

Ingredients:

For the Green Goddess Dressing:

- 1 cup fresh spinach leaves
- 1/2 cup fresh basil leaves
- 1/4 cup fresh parsley leaves
- 2 tablespoons chopped chives or green onions
- 1/4 cup plain Greek yogurt (or vegan yogurt for a dairy-free option)
- 1 tablespoon lemon juice
- 1 clove garlic, minced
- 2 tablespoons extra-virgin olive oil
- Salt and pepper, to taste
- Water, as needed to adjust consistency

For the Bowl:

- Cooked quinoa or brown rice
- Steamed broccoli florets
- Sautéed kale or spinach
- Sliced cucumber
- Sliced avocado
- Cooked chickpeas or grilled tofu
- Optional toppings: pumpkin seeds, sunflower seeds, hemp seeds

Instructions:

1. Prepare the Green Goddess Dressing:

    1. In a blender or food processor, combine fresh spinach leaves, basil leaves, parsley leaves, chopped chives or green onions, Greek yogurt (or vegan yogurt), lemon juice, minced garlic, extra-virgin olive oil, salt, and pepper.
    2. Blend until smooth and creamy. Add water a tablespoon at a time to thin out the dressing to your desired consistency. Adjust seasoning to taste.

2. Assemble the Green Goddess Bowl:

    1. Divide cooked quinoa or brown rice among serving bowls.
    2. Arrange steamed broccoli florets, sautéed kale or spinach, sliced cucumber, sliced avocado, and cooked chickpeas or grilled tofu on top of the grains.

3. Drizzle with Green Goddess Dressing:

    1. Drizzle the prepared green goddess dressing over each bowl.
    2. Optionally, sprinkle with pumpkin seeds, sunflower seeds, or hemp seeds for added crunch and nutrition.

4. Serve and Enjoy!

    - Serve the Green Goddess Bowl immediately and enjoy the fresh and vibrant flavors of the green goddess dressing paired with wholesome grains, vegetables, and protein.

Tips:

- Protein Options: Feel free to add your favorite protein sources such as grilled chicken, shrimp, salmon, or tempeh for added protein.
- Variations: Customize the bowl with any of your favorite green vegetables such as zucchini, snap peas, or green beans.
- Make It Vegan: Use vegan yogurt in the dressing and ensure all other ingredients are vegan-friendly.
- Meal Prep: Prepare the dressing and cook the grains and vegetables ahead of time, then assemble the bowls when ready to eat.

This Green Goddess Bowl is a nutritious and satisfying meal that's perfect for a quick and easy lunch or dinner. Enjoy the creamy and herbaceous flavors of the green goddess dressing paired with a variety of greens, grains, and protein in this delicious bowl!

Green Goddess Bowl

Ingredients:

For the Green Goddess Dressing:

- 1 cup fresh spinach leaves
- 1/2 cup fresh parsley leaves
- 1/4 cup fresh basil leaves
- 1/4 cup plain Greek yogurt (or dairy-free yogurt for vegan option)
- 2 tablespoons lemon juice
- 1 clove garlic, minced
- 2 tablespoons extra-virgin olive oil
- Salt and pepper, to taste
- Water, as needed to adjust consistency

For the Bowl:

- Cooked quinoa or brown rice
- Sautéed or roasted mixed vegetables (such as broccoli, zucchini, bell peppers, and cherry tomatoes)
- Sliced avocado
- Cooked chickpeas or white beans
- Optional toppings: sliced cucumber, shredded carrots, sliced radishes, pumpkin seeds, sunflower seeds

Instructions:

1. Prepare the Green Goddess Dressing:

   1. In a blender or food processor, combine fresh spinach, parsley, basil, Greek yogurt (or dairy-free yogurt), lemon juice, minced garlic, olive oil, salt, and pepper.
   2. Blend until smooth and creamy. If the dressing is too thick, add water a tablespoon at a time until desired consistency is reached. Adjust seasoning to taste.

2. Assemble the Green Goddess Bowl:

   1. Divide cooked quinoa or brown rice among serving bowls.
   2. Top the grains with sautéed or roasted mixed vegetables, sliced avocado, and cooked chickpeas or white beans.

3. Add any additional toppings you like, such as sliced cucumber, shredded carrots, sliced radishes, pumpkin seeds, or sunflower seeds.

3. Drizzle with Green Goddess Dressing:

   1. Drizzle the prepared green goddess dressing over each bowl, ensuring everything is evenly coated.

4. Serve and Enjoy!

   - Serve the Green Goddess Bowl immediately and enjoy the delicious combination of flavors and textures.

Tips:

- Protein Options: Add grilled tofu, tempeh, or sliced grilled chicken for extra protein.
- Variations: Feel free to customize the bowl with your favorite seasonal vegetables and toppings.
- Make It Vegan: Use dairy-free yogurt in the dressing and ensure all other ingredients are vegan-friendly.
- Meal Prep: Cook the grains and vegetables ahead of time, and prepare the dressing. Assemble the bowls when ready to eat for a quick and convenient meal.

This Green Goddess Bowl is a fantastic way to enjoy a variety of fresh vegetables and nutrient-packed ingredients with a creamy and flavorful dressing. It's perfect for a healthy lunch or dinner that satisfies both your taste buds and your nutritional needs!

Burrito Bowl

Ingredients:

For the Cilantro Lime Rice:

- 1 cup long-grain white rice
- 2 cups water
- 1 tablespoon olive oil
- Juice of 1 lime
- 1/4 cup chopped fresh cilantro
- Salt, to taste

For the Black Beans:

- 1 can (15 oz) black beans, drained and rinsed
- 1 clove garlic, minced
- 1 teaspoon ground cumin
- Salt and pepper, to taste

For the Grilled Fajita Veggies:

- 1 red bell pepper, sliced
- 1 green bell pepper, sliced
- 1 onion, sliced
- 2 tablespoons olive oil
- 1 teaspoon chili powder
- Salt and pepper, to taste

For Assembling the Bowl:

- Sliced avocado or guacamole
- Salsa or pico de gallo
- Shredded lettuce or cabbage
- Chopped fresh tomatoes
- Sliced jalapeños (optional)
- Sour cream or Greek yogurt (optional, for serving)
- Shredded cheese (such as cheddar or Monterey Jack, optional)
- Lime wedges, for garnish

Instructions:

1. Prepare the Cilantro Lime Rice:
    1. Rinse the rice under cold water until the water runs clear.
    2. In a pot, combine the rice, water, and olive oil. Bring to a boil over high heat.
    3. Reduce the heat to low, cover, and simmer for 15-20 minutes, or until the rice is cooked and the water is absorbed.
    4. Once cooked, fluff the rice with a fork and stir in lime juice, chopped cilantro, and salt. Set aside.

2. Prepare the Black Beans:
    1. In a saucepan, heat olive oil over medium heat. Add minced garlic and cook for 1 minute until fragrant.
    2. Add black beans, ground cumin, salt, and pepper. Stir well and cook for 5-7 minutes until heated through. Mash some of the beans with a fork for a thicker consistency if desired. Set aside.

3. Grill the Fajita Veggies:
    1. In a large skillet or grill pan, heat olive oil over medium-high heat.
    2. Add sliced bell peppers and onions to the skillet.
    3. Season with chili powder, salt, and pepper. Sauté or grill for 8-10 minutes, stirring occasionally, until the veggies are tender and slightly charred. Set aside.

4. Assemble the Burrito Bowl:
    1. Divide the cilantro lime rice, black beans, grilled fajita veggies, sliced avocado or guacamole, salsa or pico de gallo, shredded lettuce or cabbage, chopped tomatoes, and sliced jalapeños (if using) among serving bowls.
    2. Top with sour cream or Greek yogurt, shredded cheese (if using), and garnish with lime wedges.

5. Serve and Enjoy!
    - Mix everything together in the bowl before eating, squeezing lime juice over the top for extra flavor.

Tips:

- Protein Options: Add grilled chicken, steak strips, shrimp, tofu, or tempeh for additional protein.
- Vegetarian/Vegan Variation: Omit dairy toppings (sour cream, cheese) and use plant-based alternatives.

- Customize: Feel free to add other toppings like corn kernels, sliced olives, or fresh cilantro.
- Meal Prep: Prepare the rice, beans, and veggies ahead of time, and assemble the bowls when ready to eat for a quick and easy meal.

This Burrito Bowl is a satisfying and versatile meal that can be customized to suit your taste preferences. Enjoy the combination of flavors and textures in each bite!

Sesame Ginger Noodle Bowl

Ingredients:

For the Sesame Ginger Sauce:

- 1/4 cup soy sauce or tamari (for gluten-free)
- 3 tablespoons rice vinegar
- 2 tablespoons sesame oil
- 2 tablespoons honey or maple syrup
- 2 tablespoons freshly grated ginger
- 2 cloves garlic, minced
- 1 tablespoon sriracha sauce (adjust to taste for spice)
- Salt and pepper, to taste

For the Noodle Bowl:

- 8 oz (225g) noodles of your choice (such as soba noodles, rice noodles, or udon noodles)
- 1 red bell pepper, thinly sliced
- 1 carrot, julienned or thinly sliced
- 1/2 cucumber, thinly sliced
- 4 green onions, thinly sliced
- 1 cup shredded cabbage or coleslaw mix
- 1/4 cup chopped fresh cilantro or parsley
- 1/4 cup roasted peanuts or cashews, chopped (optional, for garnish)
- Sesame seeds, for garnish
- Lime wedges, for serving

Instructions:

1. Cook the Noodles:

   1. Cook the noodles according to package instructions until al dente.
   2. Drain and rinse the noodles under cold water to stop the cooking process. Set aside.

2. Prepare the Sesame Ginger Sauce:

   1. In a small bowl, whisk together soy sauce or tamari, rice vinegar, sesame oil, honey or maple syrup, freshly grated ginger, minced garlic, sriracha sauce, salt, and pepper. Adjust seasoning to taste.

3. Assemble the Sesame Ginger Noodle Bowl:

   1. In a large mixing bowl, combine the cooked noodles, sliced red bell pepper, julienned carrot, sliced cucumber, green onions, shredded cabbage or coleslaw mix, and chopped fresh cilantro or parsley.
   2. Pour the sesame ginger sauce over the noodle and vegetable mixture. Toss until everything is well coated in the sauce.

4. Serve the Sesame Ginger Noodle Bowl:

   1. Divide the noodle mixture into serving bowls.
   2. Garnish each bowl with chopped roasted peanuts or cashews (if using), sesame seeds, and a lime wedge on the side.

5. Enjoy!

   - Serve the Sesame Ginger Noodle Bowl immediately, squeezing lime juice over the noodles before eating.

Tips:

- Protein Options: Add grilled chicken, shrimp, tofu, or edamame to make it a complete meal.
- Vegetarian/Vegan Variation: Use tamari instead of soy sauce, and substitute honey with maple syrup for a vegan option.
- Customize: Feel free to add other vegetables like snap peas, broccoli florets, or bean sprouts.
- Make It Spicy: Adjust the amount of sriracha sauce to your preferred level of spice.
- Meal Prep: Prepare the sauce and chop the vegetables ahead of time for a quick and easy meal assembly.

This Sesame Ginger Noodle Bowl is a delicious and versatile dish that can be enjoyed as a light lunch or dinner. It's packed with flavors and textures that are sure to satisfy your taste buds! Adjust the ingredients and toppings according to your preferences for a personalized bowl of goodness.

Spicy Peanut Tempeh Bowl

Ingredients:

For the Spicy Peanut Tempeh:

- 8 oz (225g) tempeh, cut into cubes or strips
- 2 tablespoons soy sauce or tamari (for gluten-free)
- 2 tablespoons rice vinegar
- 1 tablespoon maple syrup or honey
- 2 cloves garlic, minced
- 1 tablespoon sriracha sauce (adjust to taste)
- 2 tablespoons peanut butter
- 2 tablespoons water
- 2 tablespoons vegetable oil, for cooking

For the Bowl:

- Cooked quinoa, brown rice, or cauliflower rice
- Sautéed or steamed vegetables (such as broccoli, bell peppers, carrots, and snap peas)
- Sliced cucumber or shredded cabbage
- Sliced green onions
- Fresh cilantro or parsley, chopped
- Lime wedges, for serving

Instructions:

1. Marinate and Cook the Tempeh:

    1. In a shallow dish, whisk together soy sauce or tamari, rice vinegar, maple syrup or honey, minced garlic, and sriracha sauce.
    2. Add the tempeh cubes or strips to the marinade, making sure they are well coated. Let marinate for at least 15-20 minutes.
    3. In a small bowl, mix together peanut butter and water to create a smooth peanut sauce.

2. Sauté the Tempeh:

    1. Heat vegetable oil in a skillet over medium-high heat.
    2. Add the marinated tempeh (reserve the marinade) and cook for 3-4 minutes on each side until golden brown and crispy.

3. Pour the reserved marinade over the tempeh in the skillet and cook for an additional 1-2 minutes, allowing the sauce to thicken and coat the tempeh.

3. Assemble the Spicy Peanut Tempeh Bowl:

   1. Divide cooked quinoa, brown rice, or cauliflower rice among serving bowls.
   2. Arrange sautéed or steamed vegetables, sliced cucumber or shredded cabbage, and cooked tempeh over the grains.
   3. Drizzle the peanut sauce over the bowl.
   4. Garnish with sliced green onions, chopped fresh cilantro or parsley, and serve with lime wedges on the side.

4. Enjoy!

   - Mix everything together in the bowl before eating, squeezing lime juice over the bowl for extra freshness and flavor.

Tips:

- Protein Options: Substitute tempeh with tofu, chickpeas, or grilled chicken if preferred.
- Vegetarian/Vegan Variation: Use maple syrup instead of honey for a vegan option.
- Customize: Feel free to add other vegetables like snap peas, shredded carrots, or bean sprouts.
- Spice Level: Adjust the amount of sriracha sauce to your preferred level of spiciness.
- Meal Prep: Marinate the tempeh ahead of time for quick assembly when ready to eat.

This Spicy Peanut Tempeh Bowl is a delicious and nutritious meal packed with protein and flavor. Enjoy the combination of spicy tempeh, peanut sauce, and fresh vegetables over grains for a satisfying and filling bowl!

Mediterranean Orzo Bowl

Ingredients:

For the Orzo Salad:

- 1 cup orzo pasta
- 1 cup cherry tomatoes, halved
- 1/2 English cucumber, diced
- 1/4 red onion, finely chopped
- 1/4 cup Kalamata olives, pitted and sliced
- 1/4 cup crumbled feta cheese (optional, omit for vegan version)
- 2 tablespoons chopped fresh parsley
- Salt and pepper, to taste

For the Dressing:

- 3 tablespoons extra-virgin olive oil
- 2 tablespoons red wine vinegar
- 1 clove garlic, minced
- 1 teaspoon dried oregano
- Salt and pepper, to taste

Optional Additions:

- Sliced grilled chicken or chickpeas for added protein
- Chopped fresh spinach or arugula
- Sliced bell peppers
- Sun-dried tomatoes

Instructions:

1. Cook the Orzo Pasta:

    1. Bring a large pot of salted water to a boil.
    2. Add the orzo pasta and cook according to package instructions until al dente.
    3. Drain the cooked orzo and rinse under cold water to stop the cooking process. Set aside.

2. Prepare the Dressing:

    1. In a small bowl, whisk together the extra-virgin olive oil, red wine vinegar, minced garlic, dried oregano, salt, and pepper until well combined. Set aside.

3. Assemble the Mediterranean Orzo Bowl:

    1. In a large mixing bowl, combine the cooked and cooled orzo pasta with cherry tomatoes, diced cucumber, finely chopped red onion, sliced Kalamata olives, crumbled feta cheese (if using), and chopped fresh parsley.
    2. Pour the dressing over the orzo salad and toss gently to combine.
    3. Season with additional salt and pepper to taste.

4. Serve and Enjoy:

    - Divide the Mediterranean Orzo Salad into serving bowls.
    - If desired, add optional additions such as sliced grilled chicken or chickpeas, chopped fresh spinach or arugula, sliced bell peppers, or sun-dried tomatoes.
    - Serve immediately and enjoy this delicious Mediterranean-inspired dish!

Tips:

- Make It Vegan: Omit the feta cheese or substitute with a vegan cheese alternative.
- Protein Options: Add grilled chicken, chickpeas, or tofu for extra protein.
- Customize: Feel free to customize the salad with your favorite Mediterranean ingredients such as artichoke hearts, roasted red peppers, or capers.
- Meal Prep: Cook the orzo and prepare the dressing ahead of time. Assemble the salad just before serving for best results.

This Mediterranean Orzo Bowl is perfect for a light and refreshing lunch or dinner. It's packed with vibrant flavors and textures that will transport you to the Mediterranean coast with every bite! Adjust the ingredients and additions based on your preferences for a personalized and satisfying meal.

Korean BBQ Tofu Bowl

Ingredients:

For the Marinated Tofu:

- 1 block (14-16 oz) firm tofu, pressed and cut into cubes
- 3 tablespoons soy sauce or tamari (for gluten-free)
- 2 tablespoons honey or maple syrup
- 1 tablespoon sesame oil
- 1 tablespoon rice vinegar
- 2 cloves garlic, minced
- 1 tablespoon grated fresh ginger
- 1 tablespoon gochujang (Korean chili paste)
- 1 tablespoon vegetable oil, for cooking

For the Bowl:

- Cooked white or brown rice
- Sautéed or stir-fried vegetables (such as bell peppers, broccoli, carrots, and snap peas)
- Sliced green onions, for garnish
- Sesame seeds, for garnish
- Kimchi, for serving (optional)

Instructions:

1. Marinate the Tofu:

    1. In a mixing bowl, whisk together soy sauce or tamari, honey or maple syrup, sesame oil, rice vinegar, minced garlic, grated ginger, and gochujang until well combined.
    2. Add the cubed tofu to the marinade, gently toss to coat, and let it marinate for at least 30 minutes, or longer if time allows.

2. Cook the Tofu:

    1. Heat vegetable oil in a large skillet or non-stick pan over medium-high heat.
    2. Add the marinated tofu cubes to the skillet in a single layer (reserve the marinade).
    3. Cook the tofu for 3-4 minutes on each side until golden and caramelized, stirring occasionally. Use a spatula to carefully flip the tofu cubes.

4. Pour the reserved marinade into the skillet and cook for an additional 1-2 minutes, allowing the sauce to thicken and coat the tofu. Remove from heat.

3. Assemble the Korean BBQ Tofu Bowl:

    1. Divide cooked rice among serving bowls.
    2. Top the rice with sautéed or stir-fried vegetables.
    3. Add the cooked Korean BBQ tofu on top of the vegetables.
    4. Garnish with sliced green onions and sesame seeds.

4. Serve and Enjoy:

    - Serve the Korean BBQ Tofu Bowl immediately, optionally with a side of kimchi for extra flavor and tanginess.

Tips:

- Tofu Preparation: Press the tofu to remove excess moisture before cutting into cubes for better texture and absorption of flavors.
- Vegetable Options: Feel free to use any of your favorite vegetables for stir-frying or sautéing in the bowl.
- Make It Spicy: Increase the amount of gochujang or add crushed red pepper flakes for extra heat.
- Customize: Customize the bowl with additional toppings like sliced avocado, pickled vegetables, or a fried egg.
- Meal Prep: Marinate the tofu ahead of time and cook it when ready to assemble the bowls for a quick and easy meal.

This Korean BBQ Tofu Bowl is a delicious and flavorful way to enjoy tofu with Korean-inspired flavors. It's a wholesome and satisfying meal that's perfect for lunch or dinner. Enjoy the bold and savory taste of this dish along with your favorite vegetables and rice!

Portobello Fajita Bowl

Ingredients:

For the Portobello Fajitas:

- 4 large portobello mushrooms, stems removed and sliced
- 3 bell peppers (any color), sliced
- 1 large onion, sliced
- 3 tablespoons olive oil
- 2 tablespoons soy sauce or tamari (for gluten-free option)
- 2 tablespoons lime juice
- 2 cloves garlic, minced
- 1 teaspoon chili powder
- 1 teaspoon ground cumin
- 1/2 teaspoon smoked paprika
- Salt and pepper, to taste

For Assembling the Bowl:

- Cooked brown rice, quinoa, or cauliflower rice
- Black beans, drained and rinsed
- Sliced avocado or guacamole
- Salsa or pico de gallo
- Chopped fresh cilantro
- Lime wedges, for serving

Instructions:

1. Marinate the Portobello Mushrooms:

   1. In a shallow dish or bowl, whisk together olive oil, soy sauce or tamari, lime juice, minced garlic, chili powder, ground cumin, smoked paprika, salt, and pepper.
   2. Add the sliced portobello mushrooms to the marinade, making sure they are well coated. Let marinate for at least 20-30 minutes.

2. Cook the Portobello Fajitas:

   1. Heat 1 tablespoon of olive oil in a large skillet or pan over medium-high heat.
   2. Add the sliced bell peppers and onion to the skillet. Sauté for 5-6 minutes until the vegetables are tender and slightly caramelized. Remove from the skillet and set aside.

3. In the same skillet, add another tablespoon of olive oil.
4. Add the marinated portobello mushrooms along with the marinade to the skillet. Cook for 6-8 minutes, stirring occasionally, until the mushrooms are tender and cooked through.

3. Assemble the Portobello Fajita Bowl:

1. Divide cooked brown rice, quinoa, or cauliflower rice among serving bowls.
2. Top with black beans, sautéed portobello fajitas, and the cooked bell peppers and onions.
3. Add sliced avocado or guacamole, salsa or pico de gallo, and chopped fresh cilantro on top.
4. Serve with lime wedges on the side for squeezing over the bowl before eating.

4. Enjoy!

- Mix everything together in the bowl before eating, squeezing lime juice over the bowl for extra flavor.

Tips:

- Grain Options: Use your favorite cooked grains or rice as the base for the bowl.
- Protein Addition: Add cooked chicken, beef strips, tofu, or tempeh for additional protein.
- Customize: Customize the bowl with your favorite toppings such as shredded lettuce, shredded cheese, sour cream, or jalapeño slices.
- Meal Prep: Marinate the portobello mushrooms and cook the vegetables ahead of time. Assemble the bowls when ready to eat for a quick and delicious meal.

This Portobello Fajita Bowl is a fantastic vegetarian dish that's packed with flavor and texture. Enjoy the savory portobello mushrooms with fajita-style vegetables and your favorite toppings for a satisfying meal that's perfect for lunch or dinner!

Beet and Quinoa Bowl

Ingredients:

For the Roasted Beets:

- 3-4 medium-sized beets, peeled and diced
- 2 tablespoons olive oil
- Salt and pepper, to taste

For the Quinoa:

- 1 cup quinoa, rinsed
- 2 cups water or vegetable broth
- Salt, to taste

For Assembling the Bowl:

- Cooked quinoa (from the above ingredients)
- Roasted beets (from the above ingredients)
- Sautéed spinach or kale
- Cooked chickpeas or black beans
- Sliced avocado
- Crumbled feta cheese or goat cheese (optional, omit for vegan version)
- Chopped fresh herbs (such as parsley or cilantro)
- Lemon wedges, for serving

For the Lemon Tahini Dressing:

- 1/4 cup tahini
- 2 tablespoons lemon juice
- 2 tablespoons water
- 1 clove garlic, minced
- Salt and pepper, to taste

Instructions:

1. Roast the Beets:

    1. Preheat the oven to 400°F (200°C).
    2. Toss the diced beets with olive oil, salt, and pepper on a baking sheet.
    3. Roast in the preheated oven for 25-30 minutes, or until the beets are tender and caramelized. Stir halfway through cooking. Remove from the oven and set aside.

2. Cook the Quinoa:

   1. Rinse the quinoa under cold water using a fine mesh sieve.
   2. In a saucepan, combine quinoa, water or vegetable broth, and a pinch of salt.
   3. Bring to a boil over medium-high heat, then reduce the heat to low, cover, and simmer for 15-20 minutes until the quinoa is cooked and fluffy. Remove from heat and let it sit covered for 5 minutes before fluffing with a fork.

3. Prepare the Lemon Tahini Dressing:

   1. In a small bowl, whisk together tahini, lemon juice, water, minced garlic, salt, and pepper until smooth and creamy. Adjust consistency with more water if needed.

4. Assemble the Beet and Quinoa Bowl:

   1. Divide cooked quinoa among serving bowls.
   2. Top with roasted beets, sautéed spinach or kale, cooked chickpeas or black beans, sliced avocado, and crumbled feta cheese or goat cheese (if using).
   3. Drizzle the lemon tahini dressing over the bowl.
   4. Garnish with chopped fresh herbs and serve with lemon wedges on the side.

5. Enjoy!

   - Mix everything together in the bowl before eating, squeezing lemon juice over the bowl for extra brightness.

Tips:

- Make-Ahead: Roast the beets and cook the quinoa ahead of time for quick assembly when ready to serve.
- Customize: Feel free to add other toppings like sliced almonds, pumpkin seeds, dried cranberries, or roasted vegetables.
- Vegan/Vegetarian: Omit the cheese for a vegan version or use vegan cheese alternatives.
- Protein Options: Add grilled tofu, tempeh, or a poached egg for additional protein.
- Meal Prep: Prepare all components separately and assemble the bowls just before serving for a fresh and delicious meal.

This Beet and Quinoa Bowl is a nutritious and satisfying dish that's perfect for a wholesome lunch or dinner. Enjoy the combination of earthy roasted beets, fluffy quinoa, and flavorful toppings with a creamy lemon tahini dressing! Adjust the ingredients and toppings according to your preferences for a personalized bowl of goodness.

Thai Green Curry Bowl

Ingredients:

For the Thai Green Curry Sauce:

- 2 tablespoons green curry paste
- 1 can (14 oz) coconut milk
- 1 tablespoon soy sauce or tamari (for gluten-free)
- 1 tablespoon brown sugar or coconut sugar
- Juice of 1 lime
- 1 tablespoon vegetable oil

For the Bowl:

- 1 block (14-16 oz) firm tofu, pressed and cubed (or use cooked chicken, shrimp, or tofu)
- 1 red bell pepper, sliced
- 1 yellow bell pepper, sliced
- 1 zucchini, sliced
- 1 cup sliced mushrooms
- 1 small eggplant, diced (optional)
- 1 can (15 oz) bamboo shoots, drained (optional)
- Cooked jasmine rice or rice noodles, for serving

Optional Garnishes:

- Fresh Thai basil leaves or cilantro
- Sliced red chili peppers
- Lime wedges

Instructions:

1. Prepare the Thai Green Curry Sauce:

    1. Heat vegetable oil in a large skillet or pot over medium heat.
    2. Add green curry paste to the skillet and sauté for 1-2 minutes until fragrant.
    3. Pour in the coconut milk, soy sauce or tamari, brown sugar or coconut sugar, and lime juice. Stir to combine.
    4. Bring the sauce to a simmer, then reduce the heat to low and let it simmer gently for 5-7 minutes, stirring occasionally. Taste and adjust seasoning if needed.

2. Cook the Tofu (or Protein) and Vegetables:
    1. In a separate skillet, heat a bit of vegetable oil over medium-high heat.
    2. Add cubed tofu (or protein of choice) to the skillet and cook until lightly browned and crispy on all sides. Remove from the skillet and set aside.
    3. In the same skillet, add sliced bell peppers, zucchini, mushrooms, eggplant (if using), and bamboo shoots (if using). Sauté for 5-7 minutes until the vegetables are tender-crisp.

3. Assemble the Thai Green Curry Bowl:
    1. Divide cooked jasmine rice or rice noodles among serving bowls.
    2. Spoon the Thai green curry sauce over the rice or noodles.
    3. Top with sautéed vegetables and cooked tofu (or protein).
    4. Garnish with fresh Thai basil leaves or cilantro, sliced red chili peppers, and lime wedges.

4. Enjoy!
    - Serve the Thai Green Curry Bowl immediately and enjoy the fragrant and flavorful Thai green curry sauce with the assortment of vegetables and protein.

Tips:

- Protein Options: Use tofu, chicken, shrimp, or your preferred protein in this dish.
- Vegetable Variations: Feel free to use any combination of vegetables you like such as snow peas, broccoli, carrots, or baby corn.
- Spice Level: Adjust the amount of green curry paste and chili peppers to your desired level of spiciness.
- Make It Vegan: Use tofu or omit the protein for a vegan version.
- Meal Prep: Prepare the curry sauce and cook the rice or noodles ahead of time. Sauté the vegetables and protein just before serving for a quick and delicious meal.

This Thai Green Curry Bowl is a comforting and flavorful dish that's perfect for a weeknight dinner. Enjoy the aromatic Thai flavors and customize the ingredients based on your preferences for a delicious homemade meal!

Harvest Grain Bowl

Ingredients:

For the Bowl:

- 1 cup cooked quinoa
- 1 cup cooked farro or barley
- 1 sweet potato, peeled and diced
- 1 cup Brussels sprouts, trimmed and halved
- 1 small red onion, sliced
- 1 tablespoon olive oil
- Salt and pepper, to taste
- 1 cup cooked chickpeas (canned or cooked from dry)
- Handful of baby spinach or mixed salad greens

For the Maple Dijon Dressing:

- 3 tablespoons olive oil
- 2 tablespoons apple cider vinegar
- 1 tablespoon Dijon mustard
- 1 tablespoon pure maple syrup
- Salt and pepper, to taste

Optional Toppings:

- Toasted pumpkin seeds or pecans
- Dried cranberries or chopped dried apricots
- Crumbled goat cheese or feta cheese (omit for vegan version)
- Sliced avocado or roasted butternut squash

Instructions:

1. Prepare the Roasted Vegetables:

    1. Preheat the oven to 400°F (200°C).
    2. Place diced sweet potato, halved Brussels sprouts, and sliced red onion on a baking sheet.
    3. Drizzle with olive oil and season with salt and pepper. Toss to coat evenly.
    4. Roast in the preheated oven for 20-25 minutes, or until vegetables are tender and caramelized. Stir halfway through cooking. Remove from the oven and set aside.

2. Make the Maple Dijon Dressing:

    1. In a small bowl, whisk together olive oil, apple cider vinegar, Dijon mustard, maple syrup, salt, and pepper until well combined. Set aside.

3. Assemble the Harvest Grain Bowl:

    1. In a large bowl or serving plate, arrange cooked quinoa and farro or barley.
    2. Top with roasted sweet potato, Brussels sprouts, red onion, and cooked chickpeas.
    3. Add a handful of baby spinach or mixed salad greens on top.

4. Drizzle with Maple Dijon Dressing:

    1. Drizzle the prepared Maple Dijon Dressing over the bowl.
    2. Optional: Add toasted pumpkin seeds or pecans, dried cranberries or chopped dried apricots, and crumbled goat cheese or feta cheese (if using).
    3. Garnish with sliced avocado or roasted butternut squash, if desired.

5. Enjoy!

    - Toss everything together gently to combine the flavors and textures before enjoying your Harvest Grain Bowl.

Tips:

- Grain Options: Feel free to use other grains such as brown rice, wild rice, or quinoa.
- Protein Additions: Substitute chickpeas with grilled chicken, tofu, or sliced hard-boiled eggs for added protein.
- Vegetable Variations: Use any seasonal vegetables you have on hand, such as roasted carrots, cauliflower, or beets.
- Make It Vegan: Omit cheese or use vegan cheese alternatives.
- Meal Prep: Prepare the grains, roasted vegetables, and dressing ahead of time. Assemble the bowls just before serving for a quick and satisfying meal.

This Harvest Grain Bowl is a nutritious and delicious meal that's perfect for lunch or dinner. Enjoy the combination of hearty grains, roasted vegetables, and flavorful dressing topped with optional toppings for added texture and taste! Adjust the ingredients based on your preferences and seasonal availability for a customized and satisfying bowl.

Vegan Taco Salad Bowl

Ingredients:

For the Taco Seasoning:

- 1 tablespoon chili powder
- 1 teaspoon ground cumin
- 1 teaspoon smoked paprika
- 1/2 teaspoon garlic powder
- 1/2 teaspoon onion powder
- 1/4 teaspoon cayenne pepper (adjust to taste)
- Salt and pepper, to taste

For the Salad Bowl:

- 1 block (14-16 oz) firm tofu, pressed and crumbled (or use cooked black beans or lentils)
- 2 tablespoons olive oil
- 1 bell pepper, diced
- 1 small red onion, diced
- 1 cup corn kernels (fresh, frozen, or canned)
- 1 can (15 oz) black beans, drained and rinsed
- 1 cup cherry tomatoes, halved
- 4 cups mixed salad greens (lettuce, spinach, or kale)
- Sliced avocado, for garnish
- Fresh cilantro, chopped, for garnish

For the Dressing:

- 1/4 cup vegan mayonnaise
- 2 tablespoons lime juice
- 1 tablespoon finely chopped cilantro
- 1 clove garlic, minced
- Salt and pepper, to taste

Optional Toppings:

- Sliced jalapeños
- Diced cucumber
- Sliced radishes
- Tortilla strips or crushed tortilla chips

Instructions:

1. Prepare the Taco Seasoning:
    1. In a small bowl, mix together chili powder, ground cumin, smoked paprika, garlic powder, onion powder, cayenne pepper, salt, and pepper. Set aside.

2. Cook the Tofu (or Beans) and Vegetables:
    1. Heat olive oil in a large skillet over medium-high heat.
    2. Add crumbled tofu (or cooked black beans) to the skillet.
    3. Sprinkle the taco seasoning over the tofu (or beans) and sauté for 5-7 minutes until heated through and slightly crispy.
    4. Add diced bell pepper, red onion, and corn kernels to the skillet. Sauté for an additional 3-4 minutes until vegetables are tender. Remove from heat.

3. Prepare the Dressing:
    1. In a small bowl, whisk together vegan mayonnaise, lime juice, chopped cilantro, minced garlic, salt, and pepper until smooth and creamy. Adjust seasoning to taste.

4. Assemble the Vegan Taco Salad Bowl:
    1. Divide mixed salad greens among serving bowls.
    2. Top with the seasoned tofu (or beans) and sautéed vegetables.
    3. Add black beans, cherry tomatoes, sliced avocado, and optional toppings such as sliced jalapeños, diced cucumber, and sliced radishes.
    4. Drizzle with the prepared dressing.
    5. Garnish with fresh cilantro and serve immediately.

5. Enjoy!
    - Toss everything together gently to combine flavors and textures before enjoying your Vegan Taco Salad Bowl.

Tips:

- Protein Options: Use crumbled tofu, cooked black beans, lentils, or chickpeas as the protein base.
- Vegetable Variations: Customize the salad with your favorite vegetables such as diced cucumber, sliced radishes, or shredded carrots.
- Make It Gluten-Free: Ensure all ingredients and seasonings are gluten-free if needed.

- Tortilla Chip Crunch: Add crunch to your salad by topping with tortilla strips or crushed tortilla chips.
- Meal Prep: Prepare the seasoned tofu (or beans) and dressing ahead of time. Assemble the bowls just before serving for a quick and delicious meal.

This Vegan Taco Salad Bowl is a delightful and nutritious meal that's packed with flavor and texture. Enjoy the zesty seasoned tofu (or beans), fresh vegetables, and creamy dressing for a satisfying lunch or dinner option! Adjust the ingredients and toppings based on your preferences for a personalized and delicious salad bowl.

Mango Salsa Rice Bowl

Ingredients:

For the Mango Salsa:

- 1 ripe mango, peeled and diced
- 1/2 red bell pepper, diced
- 1/4 cup diced red onion
- 1 jalapeño pepper, seeded and minced (optional for spice)
- Juice of 1 lime
- 2 tablespoons chopped fresh cilantro
- Salt and pepper, to taste

For the Rice Bowl:

- 1 cup cooked white or brown rice
- 1 can (15 oz) black beans, drained and rinsed
- 1 avocado, sliced
- 1/4 cup chopped fresh cilantro
- Lime wedges, for serving

Instructions:

1. Prepare the Mango Salsa:

    1. In a mixing bowl, combine diced mango, diced red bell pepper, diced red onion, minced jalapeño (if using), lime juice, chopped cilantro, salt, and pepper.
    2. Stir well to combine. Taste and adjust seasoning as needed. Set aside.

2. Assemble the Mango Salsa Rice Bowl:

    1. Divide cooked rice among serving bowls.
    2. Top each bowl with black beans, sliced avocado, and a generous portion of mango salsa.
    3. Garnish with chopped fresh cilantro and serve with lime wedges on the side.

3. Enjoy!

    - Mix everything together in the bowl before eating, squeezing lime juice over the bowl for extra freshness.

Tips:

- Rice Options: Use your favorite type of rice such as jasmine rice, basmati rice, or brown rice.
- Protein Addition: Add grilled tofu, seasoned tempeh, or grilled chicken for additional protein.
- Variations: Customize the bowl with additional toppings like diced cucumber, cherry tomatoes, or shredded lettuce.
- Make It Spicy: Adjust the amount of jalapeño pepper to your preferred level of spiciness.
- Meal Prep: Prepare the mango salsa ahead of time and assemble the rice bowls just before serving for a quick and satisfying meal.

This Mango Salsa Rice Bowl is a refreshing and delicious meal that's perfect for lunch or dinner. Enjoy the sweet and tangy flavors of mango salsa paired with creamy avocado, black beans, and seasoned rice for a satisfying and colorful bowl! Adjust the ingredients and toppings based on your preferences for a personalized and enjoyable meal.

Caprese Salad Bowl

Ingredients:

For the Salad Bowl:

- 2 cups cherry tomatoes, halved
- 8 oz fresh mozzarella cheese, cubed (or use mini mozzarella balls)
- 1 cup fresh basil leaves, torn
- 1 avocado, sliced
- Mixed salad greens (such as arugula or spinach)

For the Balsamic Glaze:

- 1/2 cup balsamic vinegar
- 1 tablespoon honey or maple syrup (optional, for sweetness)

Optional Additions:

- Sliced cucumber
- Kalamata olives
- Cooked quinoa or couscous for a heartier bowl

Instructions:

1. Prepare the Balsamic Glaze:
    1. In a small saucepan, combine balsamic vinegar and honey (if using).
    2. Bring to a simmer over medium heat, then reduce the heat to low.
    3. Let it simmer gently for 10-15 minutes until the vinegar has thickened and reduced to a syrupy consistency. Stir occasionally. Remove from heat and set aside to cool.

2. Assemble the Caprese Salad Bowl:
    1. In a large bowl or individual serving bowls, arrange mixed salad greens as the base.
    2. Arrange cherry tomatoes, fresh mozzarella cheese cubes (or balls), torn basil leaves, and sliced avocado on top of the greens.
    3. Optional: Add sliced cucumber or Kalamata olives for extra flavor and texture.
    4. Drizzle the prepared balsamic glaze over the salad bowl.

3. Enjoy!

- Serve the Caprese Salad Bowl immediately and enjoy the fresh and vibrant flavors of tomatoes, mozzarella, basil, and balsamic glaze.

Tips:

- Cheese Variation: Use fresh burrata cheese or vegan mozzarella for a dairy-free version.
- Protein Addition: Add grilled chicken, chickpeas, or cooked shrimp for added protein.
- Customize: Feel free to customize the salad with additional toppings like pine nuts, sun-dried tomatoes, or grilled vegetables.
- Make It Vegan: Use vegan mozzarella cheese or omit the cheese altogether for a vegan-friendly version.
- Meal Prep: Prepare the balsamic glaze ahead of time and assemble the salad bowls just before serving for a quick and delicious meal.

This Caprese Salad Bowl is a light and refreshing dish that's perfect for a quick lunch or dinner. Enjoy the combination of ripe tomatoes, creamy mozzarella, aromatic basil, and sweet balsamic glaze for a satisfying and flavorful salad bowl! Adjust the ingredients and toppings based on your preferences for a personalized and enjoyable meal.

Mexican Street Corn Bowl

Ingredients:

For the Bowl:

- 4 ears of corn, husked
- 1 tablespoon olive oil
- Salt and pepper, to taste
- 1 cup cooked quinoa or rice
- 1 can (15 oz) black beans, drained and rinsed
- 1 avocado, sliced
- Crumbled cotija cheese or feta cheese (omit for vegan version)
- Chopped fresh cilantro, for garnish
- Lime wedges, for serving

For the Chipotle Lime Crema:

- 1/2 cup vegan sour cream or regular sour cream
- 1 tablespoon lime juice
- 1 chipotle pepper in adobo sauce, minced
- 1/2 teaspoon smoked paprika
- Salt, to taste

Instructions:

1. Prepare the Corn:
    1. Preheat the grill or grill pan over medium-high heat.
    2. Brush the ears of corn with olive oil and season with salt and pepper.
    3. Grill the corn for about 8-10 minutes, turning occasionally, until charred and cooked through. Remove from the grill and let it cool slightly.
    4. Once cooled, cut the corn kernels off the cob using a sharp knife. Set aside.

2. Make the Chipotle Lime Crema:
    1. In a small bowl, whisk together vegan sour cream or regular sour cream, lime juice, minced chipotle pepper, smoked paprika, and salt until smooth and well combined. Adjust seasoning to taste. Set aside.

3. Assemble the Mexican Street Corn Bowl:
    1. Divide cooked quinoa or rice among serving bowls.

2. Top with grilled corn kernels, black beans, sliced avocado, and crumbled cotija cheese or feta cheese (if using).
3. Drizzle with chipotle lime crema sauce.
4. Garnish with chopped fresh cilantro and serve with lime wedges on the side.

4. Enjoy!

- Mix everything together in the bowl before eating, squeezing lime juice over the bowl for extra freshness.

Tips:

- Grain Options: Use your preferred grain such as quinoa, rice, or cauliflower rice as the base for the bowl.
- Protein Additions: Add grilled chicken, shrimp, or tofu for added protein.
- Customize: Feel free to add diced tomatoes, sliced jalapeños, or chopped red onion for extra flavor and texture.
- Make It Vegan: Use vegan sour cream and omit the cheese or use a vegan cheese alternative.
- Meal Prep: Prepare the corn and chipotle lime crema ahead of time. Assemble the bowls just before serving for a quick and delicious meal.

This Mexican Street Corn Bowl is a delightful and flavorful dish that's perfect for a summer meal or anytime you crave the delicious flavors of Mexican street corn. Enjoy the combination of grilled corn, creamy chipotle lime crema, avocado, and other toppings for a satisfying and delicious bowl! Adjust the ingredients and toppings based on your preferences for a personalized and enjoyable meal.

Spinach and Artichoke Quinoa Bowl

Ingredients:

For the Quinoa:

- 1 cup quinoa, rinsed
- 2 cups vegetable broth or water
- Salt, to taste

For the Spinach and Artichoke Mixture:

- 1 tablespoon olive oil
- 3 cloves garlic, minced
- 1 can (14 oz) artichoke hearts, drained and chopped
- 4 cups fresh spinach leaves
- Salt and pepper, to taste
- 1/2 cup grated Parmesan cheese (or nutritional yeast for vegan option)
- 1/4 cup plain Greek yogurt or vegan yogurt

Optional Additions:

- Sliced cherry tomatoes
- Sliced black olives
- Chopped fresh basil or parsley

Instructions:

1. Cook the Quinoa:

    1. In a saucepan, combine quinoa, vegetable broth or water, and a pinch of salt.
    2. Bring to a boil over medium-high heat, then reduce the heat to low, cover, and simmer for 15-20 minutes until the quinoa is cooked and fluffy. Remove from heat and fluff with a fork.

2. Prepare the Spinach and Artichoke Mixture:

    1. In a large skillet, heat olive oil over medium heat.
    2. Add minced garlic and sauté for about 1 minute until fragrant.
    3. Add chopped artichoke hearts to the skillet and cook for 3-4 minutes until lightly browned.
    4. Add fresh spinach leaves to the skillet and cook for 2-3 minutes until wilted.
    5. Season with salt and pepper to taste.

3. Combine Quinoa with Spinach and Artichoke Mixture:
    1. Add the cooked quinoa to the skillet with the spinach and artichoke mixture.
    2. Stir in grated Parmesan cheese (or nutritional yeast) and Greek yogurt (or vegan yogurt) until everything is well combined and creamy.
    3. Cook for an additional 1-2 minutes until heated through.

4. Assemble the Spinach and Artichoke Quinoa Bowl:
    1. Divide the creamy quinoa mixture into serving bowls.
    2. Top with optional additions like sliced cherry tomatoes, black olives, and chopped fresh herbs (basil or parsley).

5. Enjoy!
    - Serve the Spinach and Artichoke Quinoa Bowl warm and enjoy the creamy and flavorful combination of spinach, artichoke, and quinoa.

Tips:

- Cheese Variation: Use vegan Parmesan cheese or nutritional yeast for a dairy-free and vegan-friendly option.
- Protein Additions: Add cooked chickpeas, grilled tofu, or shredded chicken for added protein.
- Make It Creamier: Increase the amount of Greek yogurt or add a splash of almond milk or coconut milk to make the quinoa mixture creamier.
- Customize: Feel free to add your favorite vegetables or toppings to personalize the bowl.
- Meal Prep: Prepare the quinoa and spinach-artichoke mixture ahead of time. Assemble the bowls just before serving for a quick and nutritious meal.

This Spinach and Artichoke Quinoa Bowl is a satisfying and wholesome meal that's perfect for lunch or dinner. Enjoy the creamy texture and savory flavors of this dish, and feel free to customize it with your favorite ingredients! Adjust the seasonings and toppings based on your preferences for a personalized and delicious quinoa bowl.

Hawaiian Poke Bowl

Ingredients:

For the Poke:

- 1 lb sushi-grade ahi tuna or salmon, cubed
- 1/4 cup soy sauce or tamari (for gluten-free)
- 1 tablespoon sesame oil
- 1 tablespoon rice vinegar
- 1 tablespoon honey or maple syrup
- 1 teaspoon grated fresh ginger
- 2 green onions, thinly sliced
- 1 tablespoon sesame seeds
- Optional: 1 teaspoon sriracha or chili garlic sauce for heat

For Assembling the Bowl:

- Cooked sushi rice or brown rice
- Sliced avocado
- Sliced cucumber
- Shredded carrots
- Edamame beans, cooked and shelled
- Seaweed salad
- Pickled ginger
- Furikake seasoning (optional)
- Lime wedges, for serving

Instructions:

1. Prepare the Poke:

   1. In a bowl, whisk together soy sauce (or tamari), sesame oil, rice vinegar, honey (or maple syrup), grated ginger, sliced green onions, sesame seeds, and sriracha (or chili garlic sauce), if using.
   2. Add the cubed ahi tuna or salmon to the bowl and gently toss to coat. Cover and refrigerate for at least 30 minutes to marinate.

2. Assemble the Poke Bowl:

   1. Divide cooked sushi rice or brown rice into serving bowls.

2. Top with marinated poke (tuna or salmon) and arrange sliced avocado, sliced cucumber, shredded carrots, and edamame beans around the bowl.
3. Add a spoonful of seaweed salad and pickled ginger to the bowl.
4. Sprinkle furikake seasoning over the poke bowl for added flavor (if desired).
5. Serve with lime wedges on the side.

3. Enjoy!

- Mix everything together in the bowl before eating, squeezing lime juice over the poke bowl for extra freshness.

Tips:

- Fish Variations: Use sushi-grade ahi tuna, salmon, or other seafood like cooked shrimp or tofu for a vegetarian version.
- Rice Options: Use your favorite rice such as sushi rice, brown rice, or cauliflower rice as the base for the poke bowl.
- Toppings: Customize the bowl with your favorite toppings such as sliced radishes, mango cubes, or jalapeño slices.
- Make It Gluten-Free: Use tamari instead of soy sauce for a gluten-free option.
- Meal Prep: Marinate the poke ahead of time and assemble the poke bowls just before serving for a quick and delicious meal.

This Hawaiian Poke Bowl is a colorful and satisfying dish that's perfect for a taste of Hawaii at home. Enjoy the fresh flavors of marinated fish, crunchy vegetables, creamy avocado, and savory toppings in this delicious and nutritious bowl! Adjust the ingredients and toppings based on your preferences for a personalized and enjoyable poke bowl experience.

Balsamic Glazed Veggie Bowl

Ingredients:

For the Balsamic Glaze:

- 1/2 cup balsamic vinegar
- 2 tablespoons honey or maple syrup
- 1 tablespoon Dijon mustard
- 2 cloves garlic, minced
- Salt and pepper, to taste

For the Roasted Vegetables:

- 1 large sweet potato, peeled and diced
- 2 bell peppers (any color), seeded and diced
- 1 red onion, sliced
- 1 zucchini, sliced
- 1 cup cherry tomatoes
- 2 tablespoons olive oil
- Salt and pepper, to taste
- Optional: Fresh herbs (such as thyme or rosemary), chopped

For Assembling the Bowl:

- Cooked quinoa or brown rice
- Baby spinach or mixed salad greens
- Avocado slices
- Crumbled feta cheese or goat cheese (omit for vegan version)
- Toasted nuts or seeds (such as pine nuts or pumpkin seeds)
- Fresh basil or parsley, chopped, for garnish

Instructions:

1. Prepare the Balsamic Glaze:

   1. In a small saucepan, combine balsamic vinegar, honey or maple syrup, Dijon mustard, minced garlic, salt, and pepper.
   2. Bring to a simmer over medium heat, then reduce the heat to low.
   3. Let it simmer gently for 10-15 minutes until the vinegar has thickened and reduced to a syrupy consistency. Stir occasionally. Remove from heat and set aside to cool.

2. Roast the Vegetables:

    1. Preheat the oven to 400°F (200°C).
    2. In a large mixing bowl, toss diced sweet potato, bell peppers, red onion, zucchini, and cherry tomatoes with olive oil, salt, pepper, and optional fresh herbs.
    3. Spread the vegetables evenly on a baking sheet.
    4. Roast in the preheated oven for 20-25 minutes, stirring halfway through, until the vegetables are tender and caramelized.

3. Assemble the Balsamic Glazed Veggie Bowl:

    1. Divide cooked quinoa or brown rice and baby spinach or mixed salad greens among serving bowls.
    2. Arrange the roasted vegetables on top of the grains and greens.
    3. Drizzle with the prepared balsamic glaze.
    4. Top with avocado slices, crumbled feta cheese or goat cheese (if using), and toasted nuts or seeds.
    5. Garnish with fresh chopped basil or parsley.

4. Enjoy!

    - Toss everything together gently in the bowl before eating to combine the flavors and textures.

Tips:

- Vegetable Variations: Feel free to use any seasonal vegetables you have on hand such as eggplant, cauliflower, or asparagus.
- Grain Options: Use your favorite grain such as quinoa, brown rice, couscous, or farro as the base for the veggie bowl.
- Make It Vegan: Omit the cheese or use a vegan cheese alternative.
- Protein Addition: Add grilled tofu, chickpeas, or lentils for added protein.
- Meal Prep: Roast the vegetables and prepare the balsamic glaze ahead of time. Assemble the bowls just before serving for a quick and delicious meal.

This Balsamic Glazed Veggie Bowl is a flavorful and nutritious dish that's perfect for a satisfying lunch or dinner. Enjoy the combination of roasted vegetables, tangy balsamic glaze, creamy avocado, and crunchy nuts for a delicious and wholesome veggie bowl! Adjust the ingredients and toppings based on your preferences for a personalized and enjoyable meal.

Cauliflower Shawarma Bowl

Ingredients:

For the Cauliflower Shawarma:

- 1 head of cauliflower, cut into florets
- 2 tablespoons olive oil
- 2 teaspoons ground cumin
- 2 teaspoons smoked paprika
- 1 teaspoon ground turmeric
- 1 teaspoon ground coriander
- 1/2 teaspoon ground cinnamon
- Salt and pepper, to taste

For the Bowl:

- Cooked quinoa or brown rice
- Mixed salad greens or baby spinach
- Cherry tomatoes, halved
- Sliced cucumber
- Sliced red onion
- Kalamata olives, pitted
- Hummus, store-bought or homemade

For the Tahini Sauce:

- 1/4 cup tahini
- 2 tablespoons lemon juice
- 2 tablespoons water
- 1 clove garlic, minced
- Salt, to taste

Optional Garnishes:

- Fresh parsley, chopped
- Sliced avocado
- Toasted pine nuts or almonds

Instructions:

1. Prepare the Cauliflower Shawarma:

1. Preheat the oven to 425°F (220°C) and line a baking sheet with parchment paper.
2. In a large bowl, toss the cauliflower florets with olive oil, ground cumin, smoked paprika, turmeric, coriander, cinnamon, salt, and pepper until well coated.
3. Spread the seasoned cauliflower in a single layer on the prepared baking sheet.
4. Roast in the preheated oven for 20-25 minutes, or until the cauliflower is tender and lightly browned, tossing halfway through cooking.

2. Make the Tahini Sauce:

1. In a small bowl, whisk together tahini, lemon juice, water, minced garlic, and salt until smooth and creamy. Add more water if needed to achieve a drizzling consistency.

3. Assemble the Cauliflower Shawarma Bowl:

1. Divide cooked quinoa or brown rice and mixed salad greens or baby spinach among serving bowls.
2. Top with roasted cauliflower shawarma, cherry tomatoes, sliced cucumber, sliced red onion, and Kalamata olives.
3. Drizzle the tahini sauce and spoon dollops of hummus over the bowl.
4. Garnish with fresh chopped parsley, sliced avocado, and toasted pine nuts or almonds, if desired.

4. Enjoy!

- Mix everything together in the bowl before eating to combine the flavors and textures.

Tips:

- Cauliflower Variation: You can also use broccoli or a mix of both cauliflower and broccoli for the shawarma.
- Grain Options: Use your favorite grain such as quinoa, brown rice, or couscous as the base for the bowl.
- Protein Addition: Add chickpeas, grilled tofu, or sliced grilled chicken for added protein.
- Customize: Feel free to add or substitute any vegetables and toppings based on your preferences.
- Meal Prep: Roast the cauliflower and prepare the tahini sauce ahead of time. Assemble the bowls just before serving for a quick and delicious meal.

This Cauliflower Shawarma Bowl is a flavorful and satisfying dish that's perfect for a healthy and delicious meal. Enjoy the combination of roasted cauliflower, tahini sauce, hummus, and fresh vegetables for a flavorful and nutrient-packed bowl! Adjust the ingredients and toppings based on your preferences for a personalized and enjoyable meal experience.

Sesame Orange Tofu Bowl

Ingredients:

For the Crispy Tofu:

- 1 block (14-16 oz) extra-firm tofu, pressed and cubed
- 2 tablespoons cornstarch or arrowroot powder
- Salt and pepper, to taste
- 2 tablespoons sesame oil, for cooking

For the Orange Sauce:

- 1/2 cup orange juice (freshly squeezed is best)
- Zest of 1 orange
- 3 tablespoons soy sauce or tamari (for gluten-free)
- 2 tablespoons rice vinegar
- 2 tablespoons honey or maple syrup
- 2 cloves garlic, minced
- 1 tablespoon grated fresh ginger
- 1 tablespoon cornstarch or arrowroot powder, mixed with 2 tablespoons water

For Assembling the Bowl:

- Cooked brown rice or quinoa
- Steamed broccoli florets
- Sliced bell peppers
- Thinly sliced green onions, for garnish
- Sesame seeds, for garnish

Instructions:

1. Prepare the Crispy Tofu:

    1. Press the block of tofu to remove excess moisture. Cut the tofu into cubes and place them in a bowl.
    2. Season the tofu cubes with salt and pepper, then toss with cornstarch or arrowroot powder until evenly coated.
    3. Heat sesame oil in a large skillet or non-stick pan over medium-high heat.
    4. Add the tofu cubes to the pan in a single layer. Cook for 4-5 minutes on each side, or until crispy and golden brown. Remove from the pan and set aside.

2. Make the Orange Sauce:

    1. In a small bowl, whisk together orange juice, orange zest, soy sauce or tamari, rice vinegar, honey or maple syrup, minced garlic, and grated ginger.
    2. Pour the mixture into a saucepan and bring to a simmer over medium heat.
    3. Add the cornstarch or arrowroot mixture to the saucepan, stirring constantly until the sauce thickens and becomes glossy. Remove from heat.

3. Assemble the Sesame Orange Tofu Bowl:

    1. Divide cooked brown rice or quinoa among serving bowls.
    2. Arrange steamed broccoli florets and sliced bell peppers around the bowl.
    3. Top with crispy tofu cubes.
    4. Drizzle the orange sauce over the tofu and vegetables.
    5. Garnish with thinly sliced green onions and sesame seeds.

4. Enjoy!

    - Mix everything together in the bowl before eating to combine the flavors and textures.

Tips:

- Tofu Preparation: Pressing the tofu before cooking helps to remove excess moisture and allows the tofu to crisp up better.
- Vegetable Variations: Feel free to use any of your favorite vegetables such as carrots, snap peas, or bok choy in the bowl.
- Make It Spicy: Add a pinch of red pepper flakes or sriracha to the orange sauce for a spicy kick.
- Meal Prep: Cook the tofu and prepare the orange sauce ahead of time. Assemble the bowls just before serving for a quick and delicious meal.

This Sesame Orange Tofu Bowl is a flavorful and satisfying dish that's perfect for a healthy lunch or dinner. Enjoy the crispy tofu coated in a sweet and tangy orange sauce, served with nutritious vegetables and grains. Customize the bowl with your favorite vegetables and toppings for a personalized and delicious meal experience!

Ratatouille Polenta Bowl

Ingredients:

For the Ratatouille:

- 1 eggplant, diced
- 2 zucchini, diced
- 1 bell pepper (any color), diced
- 1 onion, diced
- 2 cloves garlic, minced
- 2 cups diced tomatoes (canned or fresh)
- 2 tablespoons tomato paste
- 1 teaspoon dried thyme
- 1 teaspoon dried oregano
- Salt and pepper, to taste
- Olive oil, for cooking

For the Creamy Polenta:

- 1 cup polenta (cornmeal)
- 4 cups vegetable broth or water
- Salt, to taste
- 2 tablespoons butter or olive oil (optional, for creaminess)

For Assembling the Bowl:

- Fresh basil leaves, chopped, for garnish
- Grated Parmesan cheese or nutritional yeast (optional, for topping)
- Red pepper flakes (optional, for heat)

Instructions:

1. Prepare the Ratatouille:

    1. Heat a large skillet or pot over medium heat. Add a drizzle of olive oil.
    2. Add the diced onion and garlic to the skillet. Sauté for 2-3 minutes until softened.
    3. Add the diced eggplant, zucchini, and bell pepper to the skillet. Cook for 8-10 minutes, stirring occasionally, until vegetables are tender.
    4. Stir in the diced tomatoes, tomato paste, dried thyme, and dried oregano.

5. Season with salt and pepper to taste. Simmer for 10-15 minutes until the flavors meld together and the ratatouille thickens slightly. Remove from heat and set aside.

2. Make the Creamy Polenta:

    1. In a medium saucepan, bring vegetable broth or water to a boil.
    2. Gradually whisk in the polenta, stirring constantly to prevent lumps.
    3. Reduce the heat to low and continue to cook, stirring frequently, for 15-20 minutes until the polenta is thick and creamy.
    4. Stir in butter or olive oil (if using) and season with salt to taste.

3. Assemble the Ratatouille Polenta Bowl:

    1. Divide the creamy polenta among serving bowls.
    2. Top each bowl with a generous portion of ratatouille.
    3. Garnish with chopped fresh basil leaves and grated Parmesan cheese or nutritional yeast, if desired.
    4. Sprinkle with red pepper flakes for a touch of heat.

4. Enjoy!

    - Serve the Ratatouille Polenta Bowl warm and enjoy the creamy polenta topped with flavorful ratatouille and fresh herbs.

Tips:

- Vegetable Variations: Feel free to add other vegetables like cherry tomatoes, mushrooms, or spinach to the ratatouille.
- Make It Vegan: Use olive oil instead of butter in the polenta, and omit the Parmesan cheese or use nutritional yeast for a vegan-friendly option.
- Protein Addition: Add cooked chickpeas, lentils, or grilled tofu on top of the bowl for added protein.
- Customize: Feel free to adjust the seasoning and spices in the ratatouille to suit your taste preferences.
- Meal Prep: Prepare the ratatouille and creamy polenta ahead of time. Assemble the bowls just before serving for a quick and delicious meal.

This Ratatouille Polenta Bowl is a comforting and flavorful dish that's perfect for a satisfying dinner. Enjoy the combination of creamy polenta with a rich and savory ratatouille for a delicious and comforting meal experience! Adjust the ingredients and toppings based on your preferences for a personalized and enjoyable bowl.

Coconut Lime Rice Bowl

Ingredients:

For the Coconut Lime Rice:

- 1 cup jasmine rice or basmati rice
- 1 cup coconut milk (canned, full-fat)
- 1 cup water
- Zest of 1 lime
- Juice of 1 lime
- 1 tablespoon coconut oil or olive oil
- Salt, to taste

For Assembling the Bowl:

- Cooked protein of your choice (such as tofu, chicken, shrimp, or chickpeas)
- Sautéed vegetables (such as bell peppers, snap peas, carrots, or broccoli)
- Sliced avocado
- Fresh cilantro, chopped
- Lime wedges, for garnish

For the Zesty Dressing:

- 2 tablespoons soy sauce or tamari (for gluten-free)
- 2 tablespoons lime juice
- 1 tablespoon honey or maple syrup
- 1 tablespoon sesame oil
- 1 clove garlic, minced
- 1 teaspoon grated fresh ginger
- Red pepper flakes, to taste (optional)

Instructions:

1. Prepare the Coconut Lime Rice:

   1. Rinse the rice under cold water until the water runs clear.
   2. In a saucepan, combine the rinsed rice, coconut milk, water, lime zest, lime juice, coconut oil or olive oil, and salt.
   3. Bring to a boil over medium-high heat, then reduce the heat to low, cover, and simmer for 15-20 minutes until the rice is cooked and the liquid is absorbed.

4. Remove from heat and let it sit covered for 5 minutes. Fluff the rice with a fork and set aside.

2. Prepare the Zesty Dressing:
   1. In a small bowl, whisk together soy sauce or tamari, lime juice, honey or maple syrup, sesame oil, minced garlic, grated ginger, and red pepper flakes (if using). Adjust seasoning to taste.

3. Assemble the Coconut Lime Rice Bowl:
   1. Divide the coconut lime rice among serving bowls.
   2. Top with cooked protein (tofu, chicken, shrimp, or chickpeas) and sautéed vegetables (bell peppers, snap peas, carrots, broccoli).
   3. Arrange sliced avocado on top of the bowl.
   4. Drizzle the zesty dressing over the bowl.
   5. Garnish with chopped fresh cilantro and serve with lime wedges on the side.

4. Enjoy!
   - Mix everything together in the bowl before eating to combine the flavors and textures. Squeeze lime wedges over the bowl for extra freshness.

Tips:

- Protein Options: Customize the bowl with your choice of protein, such as tofu, chicken, shrimp, or chickpeas.
- Vegetable Variations: Use any vegetables you have on hand for the sautéed vegetables, such as bell peppers, snap peas, carrots, broccoli, or mushrooms.
- Make It Vegan: Use tofu, chickpeas, or vegetables as the protein, and replace honey with maple syrup in the dressing for a vegan-friendly option.
- Customize: Feel free to add additional toppings such as sliced cucumber, cherry tomatoes, or roasted nuts for extra flavor and texture.
- Meal Prep: Prepare the coconut lime rice and zesty dressing ahead of time. Assemble the bowls just before serving for a quick and delicious meal.

This Coconut Lime Rice Bowl is a flavorful and satisfying dish that's perfect for a quick and healthy meal. Enjoy the fragrant coconut lime rice with your favorite protein, vegetables, and zesty dressing for a delicious and balanced bowl! Adjust the ingredients and toppings based on your preferences for a personalized and enjoyable meal experience.

Vegan Cobb Salad Bowl

Ingredients:

For the Salad:

- Mixed salad greens (lettuce, spinach, arugula, or your choice)
- 1 cup cooked quinoa or grains of choice (such as farro, bulgur, or brown rice)
- 1 cup cherry tomatoes, halved
- 1 cucumber, diced
- 1 cup cooked chickpeas or black beans
- 1 cup cooked corn kernels
- 1 avocado, sliced
- 1 cup diced bell peppers (any color)
- 1/2 cup sliced black olives
- 1/4 cup chopped red onion
- Fresh herbs (such as parsley or cilantro), chopped

For the Vegan "Bacon" Bits (optional):

- 1 cup coconut flakes (unsweetened)
- 1 tablespoon soy sauce or tamari
- 1 tablespoon maple syrup
- 1/2 teaspoon smoked paprika
- Pinch of black pepper

For the Creamy Vegan Dressing:

- 1/2 cup vegan mayonnaise
- 2 tablespoons apple cider vinegar or lemon juice
- 1 tablespoon Dijon mustard
- 1 clove garlic, minced
- 1 tablespoon chopped fresh chives or green onions
- Salt and pepper, to taste
- Water, as needed to adjust consistency

Instructions:

1. Prepare the Vegan "Bacon" Bits (optional):

   1. Preheat the oven to 325°F (160°C) and line a baking sheet with parchment paper.

2. In a bowl, combine coconut flakes, soy sauce or tamari, maple syrup, smoked paprika, and black pepper. Mix well to coat the coconut flakes.
3. Spread the coated coconut flakes evenly on the prepared baking sheet.
4. Bake for 10-15 minutes, stirring occasionally, until the coconut flakes are crispy and golden brown. Watch closely to prevent burning. Remove from the oven and set aside to cool.

2. Make the Creamy Vegan Dressing:

1. In a small bowl, whisk together vegan mayonnaise, apple cider vinegar or lemon juice, Dijon mustard, minced garlic, chopped chives or green onions, salt, and pepper.
2. Adjust the consistency of the dressing by adding water, a little at a time, until desired thickness is reached. Taste and adjust seasoning as needed.

3. Assemble the Vegan Cobb Salad Bowl:

1. Arrange mixed salad greens in a large serving bowl or individual bowls.
2. Arrange cooked quinoa or grains, cherry tomatoes, diced cucumber, cooked chickpeas or black beans, cooked corn kernels, sliced avocado, diced bell peppers, sliced black olives, and chopped red onion on top of the greens.
3. Sprinkle the crispy vegan "bacon" bits (if using) and chopped fresh herbs over the salad.
4. Drizzle the creamy vegan dressing over the salad just before serving.

4. Enjoy!

- Toss everything together gently in the bowl before eating to combine the flavors and textures.

Tips:

- Customize Your Toppings: Feel free to add or substitute any of your favorite vegetables and protein sources in the salad.
- Make It Gluten-Free: Ensure that all ingredients used are gluten-free, especially the grains and soy sauce or tamari.
- Prep Ahead: Cook the quinoa or grains, chop the vegetables, and make the dressing in advance for quicker assembly.
- Protein Options: Experiment with different plant-based protein sources such as tempeh, tofu, or lentils for variety.
- Storage: Store any leftover salad components separately in the refrigerator and assemble just before serving to keep the salad fresh.

This Vegan Cobb Salad Bowl is a colorful and satisfying meal that's perfect for lunch or dinner. Enjoy the combination of fresh greens, protein-rich ingredients, and creamy dressing for a delicious and nutritious salad bowl experience! Adjust the ingredients and toppings based on your preferences to create your own version of this vegan Cobb salad.

Chipotle Sweet Potato Bowl

Ingredients:

For the Chipotle Roasted Sweet Potatoes:

- 2 large sweet potatoes, peeled and cubed
- 2 tablespoons olive oil
- 2 teaspoons chipotle chili powder (adjust to taste)
- 1 teaspoon smoked paprika
- 1 teaspoon garlic powder
- Salt and pepper, to taste

For the Bowl:

- Cooked quinoa or brown rice
- Cooked black beans or pinto beans
- Sautéed bell peppers and onions
- Fresh corn kernels (cooked or raw)
- Sliced avocado
- Chopped fresh cilantro, for garnish
- Lime wedges, for serving

For the Chipotle Lime Dressing:

- 1/3 cup plain Greek yogurt or dairy-free yogurt
- 2 tablespoons lime juice
- 1 tablespoon adobo sauce (from canned chipotle peppers)
- 1 teaspoon honey or maple syrup
- 1/2 teaspoon ground cumin
- Salt and pepper, to taste
- Water, as needed to adjust consistency

Instructions:

1. Prepare the Chipotle Roasted Sweet Potatoes:

    1. Preheat the oven to 400°F (200°C) and line a baking sheet with parchment paper.
    2. In a bowl, toss the cubed sweet potatoes with olive oil, chipotle chili powder, smoked paprika, garlic powder, salt, and pepper until evenly coated.
    3. Spread the sweet potatoes in a single layer on the prepared baking sheet.

4. Roast in the preheated oven for 25-30 minutes, tossing halfway through, until the sweet potatoes are tender and caramelized. Remove from the oven and set aside.

2. Make the Chipotle Lime Dressing:

   1. In a small bowl, whisk together Greek yogurt (or dairy-free yogurt), lime juice, adobo sauce, honey or maple syrup, ground cumin, salt, and pepper.
   2. Adjust the consistency of the dressing by adding water, a little at a time, until desired thickness is reached. Taste and adjust seasoning as needed.

3. Assemble the Chipotle Sweet Potato Bowl:

   1. Divide cooked quinoa or brown rice among serving bowls.
   2. Top with roasted chipotle sweet potatoes, cooked black beans or pinto beans, sautéed bell peppers and onions, fresh corn kernels, and sliced avocado.
   3. Drizzle the chipotle lime dressing over the bowl.
   4. Garnish with chopped fresh cilantro and serve with lime wedges on the side.

4. Enjoy!

   - Mix everything together in the bowl before eating to combine the flavors and textures. Squeeze lime wedges over the bowl for extra freshness.

Tips:

- Customize Your Bowl: Feel free to add or substitute any of your favorite ingredients such as grilled tofu, roasted vegetables, or greens like spinach or kale.
- Make It Spicy: Increase the amount of chipotle chili powder or adobo sauce for a spicier dressing.
- Prep Ahead: Cook the quinoa or rice, roast the sweet potatoes, and prepare the dressing in advance for quicker assembly.
- Protein Options: Experiment with different protein sources such as grilled chicken, shrimp, or tempeh for variation.
- Storage: Store any leftover components separately in the refrigerator and assemble just before serving to keep the bowl fresh.

This Chipotle Sweet Potato Bowl is a delicious and nutritious meal that's perfect for a quick lunch or dinner. Enjoy the smoky and spicy flavors of roasted sweet potatoes with protein, veggies, and a zesty chipotle lime dressing for a satisfying bowl experience!

Adjust the ingredients and toppings based on your preferences to create your own version of this flavorful bowl.

Mediterranean Stuffed Pepper Bowl

Ingredients:

For the Stuffed Peppers:

- 4 large bell peppers (any color), tops cut off and seeds removed
- 1 cup cooked quinoa or couscous
- 1 can (15 oz) chickpeas, drained and rinsed
- 1 cup cherry tomatoes, halved
- 1/2 English cucumber, diced
- 1/4 cup pitted Kalamata olives, sliced
- 1/4 cup chopped fresh parsley
- 1/4 cup crumbled feta cheese (optional, omit for vegan version)
- 2 tablespoons extra-virgin olive oil
- 2 tablespoons lemon juice
- 1 teaspoon dried oregano
- Salt and pepper, to taste

For Serving:

- Mixed salad greens or baby spinach
- Hummus, store-bought or homemade
- Lemon wedges, for serving
- Additional fresh herbs for garnish (such as mint or basil)

Instructions:

1. Prepare the Stuffed Peppers:

   1. Preheat the oven to 375°F (190°C). Place the hollowed-out bell peppers in a baking dish.
   2. In a large bowl, combine cooked quinoa or couscous, chickpeas, cherry tomatoes, diced cucumber, sliced olives, chopped parsley, and crumbled feta cheese (if using).
   3. In a small bowl, whisk together extra-virgin olive oil, lemon juice, dried oregano, salt, and pepper.
   4. Pour the dressing over the quinoa mixture and toss until well combined.
   5. Spoon the quinoa mixture evenly into the bell peppers, pressing down gently to fill.

2. Bake the Stuffed Peppers:

1. Cover the baking dish with foil and bake in the preheated oven for 25-30 minutes, or until the peppers are tender.
2. Remove the foil and bake for an additional 5-10 minutes to lightly brown the tops of the peppers.

3. Assemble the Mediterranean Stuffed Pepper Bowls:

   1. Arrange mixed salad greens or baby spinach in serving bowls.
   2. Place a baked stuffed pepper on top of the greens.
   3. Spoon a dollop of hummus beside each stuffed pepper.
   4. Garnish with additional fresh herbs and serve with lemon wedges on the side.

4. Enjoy!

   - Serve the Mediterranean Stuffed Pepper Bowls warm, with extra lemon wedges for squeezing over the peppers.

Tips:

- Variations: Feel free to customize the filling with other Mediterranean ingredients such as artichoke hearts, sun-dried tomatoes, or pine nuts.
- Make It Vegan: Omit the feta cheese or replace it with a vegan alternative.
- Protein Options: Add grilled tofu, chickpeas, or lentils to the filling for extra protein.
- Prep Ahead: Prepare the filling and stuff the peppers in advance. Store them in the refrigerator until ready to bake.
- Storage: Store any leftover stuffed pepper filling separately in the refrigerator and assemble fresh bowls as needed.

This Mediterranean Stuffed Pepper Bowl is a delicious and wholesome meal that's perfect for lunch or dinner. Enjoy the vibrant flavors of the Mediterranean with stuffed peppers filled with quinoa, chickpeas, vegetables, and herbs, served over greens and topped with hummus. Customize the ingredients based on your preferences for a personalized and satisfying bowl experience!

Teriyaki Mushroom Bowl

Ingredients:

For the Teriyaki Mushrooms:

- 1 pound (450g) mushrooms (such as button mushrooms, cremini, or shiitake), sliced
- 3 tablespoons soy sauce or tamari (for gluten-free)
- 2 tablespoons rice vinegar
- 2 tablespoons mirin (Japanese sweet rice wine) or maple syrup
- 2 cloves garlic, minced
- 1-inch piece of ginger, grated
- 2 tablespoons vegetable oil (for cooking)
- Sesame seeds, for garnish
- Sliced green onions, for garnish

For the Bowl:

- Cooked white or brown rice
- Steamed broccoli florets
- Sliced bell peppers (any color)
- Sliced carrots
- Sautéed spinach or kale
- Optional: Sliced avocado, shredded cabbage, edamame

Instructions:

1. Prepare the Teriyaki Mushrooms:

   1. In a bowl, whisk together soy sauce or tamari, rice vinegar, mirin or maple syrup, minced garlic, and grated ginger to make the teriyaki sauce.
   2. Heat vegetable oil in a large skillet or wok over medium-high heat.
   3. Add the sliced mushrooms to the skillet and sauté for 5-6 minutes until they start to brown and release their juices.
   4. Pour the teriyaki sauce over the mushrooms and stir well to coat.
   5. Continue to cook for another 3-4 minutes, stirring frequently, until the mushrooms are tender and glazed with the sauce. Remove from heat.

2. Assemble the Teriyaki Mushroom Bowl:

   1. Divide cooked rice among serving bowls.

2. Arrange steamed broccoli florets, sliced bell peppers, sliced carrots, and sautéed spinach or kale around the rice.
3. Spoon the teriyaki mushrooms over the rice and vegetables.
4. Garnish with sesame seeds and sliced green onions.

3. Enjoy!

- Serve the Teriyaki Mushroom Bowl warm and enjoy the savory teriyaki-glazed mushrooms with the rice and vegetables.

Tips:

- Variations: Feel free to add or substitute different vegetables such as snap peas, bok choy, or snow peas.
- Protein Options: Add tofu, tempeh, or edamame to the bowl for added protein.
- Make It Gluten-Free: Use gluten-free tamari instead of soy sauce.
- Prep Ahead: Cook the rice and prepare the teriyaki sauce in advance. Sauté the mushrooms just before assembling the bowls.
- Customize: Adjust the sweetness and saltiness of the teriyaki sauce to suit your taste preferences.

This Teriyaki Mushroom Bowl is a delicious and satisfying meal that's perfect for a quick and flavorful dinner. Enjoy the umami-rich teriyaki mushrooms served over rice and a variety of fresh vegetables. Customize the bowl with your favorite veggies and toppings for a personalized and nutritious meal experience!

Curried Chickpea Couscous Bowl

Ingredients:

For the Curried Chickpeas:

- 1 can (15 oz) chickpeas (garbanzo beans), drained and rinsed
- 1 tablespoon olive oil
- 1 onion, finely chopped
- 3 cloves garlic, minced
- 1 tablespoon curry powder
- 1 teaspoon ground cumin
- 1/2 teaspoon turmeric powder
- 1/4 teaspoon cayenne pepper (adjust to taste)
- Salt and pepper, to taste
- 1 can (14 oz) diced tomatoes, with juices
- 1/2 cup vegetable broth or water

For the Couscous:

- 1 cup couscous
- 1 cup vegetable broth or water
- 1 tablespoon olive oil
- Salt, to taste

For Assembling the Bowl:

- Chopped fresh vegetables (such as cucumber, cherry tomatoes, bell peppers)
- Fresh spinach or mixed salad greens
- Sliced avocado
- Fresh cilantro or parsley, chopped
- Lemon wedges, for serving

Instructions:

1. Prepare the Curried Chickpeas:

    1. Heat olive oil in a large skillet or pan over medium heat.
    2. Add chopped onion and sauté until translucent, about 3-4 minutes.
    3. Add minced garlic, curry powder, ground cumin, turmeric, cayenne pepper, salt, and pepper. Stir and cook for 1 minute until fragrant.
    4. Add drained chickpeas to the skillet and stir to coat with the spices.

5. Pour in diced tomatoes with their juices and vegetable broth or water. Stir well to combine.
6. Bring the mixture to a simmer, then reduce heat to low and let it cook for 10-15 minutes, stirring occasionally, until the sauce thickens slightly and the flavors meld together. Adjust seasoning if needed.

2. Prepare the Couscous:

1. In a small saucepan, bring vegetable broth or water and olive oil to a boil.
2. Stir in couscous and a pinch of salt. Remove from heat, cover with a lid, and let it sit for 5 minutes.
3. Fluff the couscous with a fork and set aside.

3. Assemble the Curried Chickpea Couscous Bowl:

1. Divide cooked couscous among serving bowls.
2. Top with curried chickpeas and any remaining sauce from the skillet.
3. Arrange chopped fresh vegetables, spinach or mixed greens, sliced avocado, and chopped fresh herbs around the couscous and chickpeas.
4. Garnish with additional fresh herbs and serve with lemon wedges on the side.

4. Enjoy!

- Mix everything together in the bowl before eating to combine the flavors and textures.
- Squeeze fresh lemon juice over the bowl for extra brightness and flavor.

Tips:

- Variations: Feel free to add other vegetables like roasted eggplant, zucchini, or carrots to the bowl.
- Protein Options: Add grilled tofu, tempeh, or sliced chicken for extra protein.
- Make It Vegan: Ensure that all ingredients used, including the vegetable broth, are vegan-friendly.
- Customize: Adjust the spices and seasonings in the curried chickpeas to suit your taste preferences.
- Prep Ahead: Prepare the curried chickpeas and couscous in advance. Store them separately in the refrigerator and assemble the bowls just before serving.

This Curried Chickpea Couscous Bowl is a delicious and satisfying meal that's perfect

for a quick lunch or dinner. Enjoy the fragrant and spicy curried chickpeas paired with fluffy couscous and fresh vegetables for a delightful bowl experience! Adjust the ingredients and toppings based on your preferences for a personalized and enjoyable dish.

www.ingramcontent.com/pod-product-compliance
Lightning Source LLC
LaVergne TN
LVHW061938070526
838199LV00060B/3867